Making Your Words Work!

Using NLP to Improve Communication, Learning & Behaviour

Terry Mahony

Crown House Publishing
www.crownhouse.co.uk
www.chpus.com

First published by

Crown House Publishing Ltd
Crown Buildings, Bancyfelin, Carmarthen, Wales, SA33 5ND, UK
www.crownhouse.co.uk

and

Crown House Publishing Ltd
6 Trowbridge Drive, Suite 5, Bedhel, CT 06801-2858, USA
www.CHPUS.com

www.crownhouse.co.uk

British Library Cataloguing-in-Publication Data
A catalogue entry for this book is available
from the British Library.

13-Digit ISBN 978-184590041-0
10-Digit ISBN 184590041-3

LCCN 2007921857

Printed and bound by
Cromwell Press, Trowbridge, Wiltshire

For Danielle and Katherine,
who both prompted and contributed to this book

Table of Contents

List of figures

List of tables

List of exercises

Acknowledgements

My thanks to the many teachers who have contributed to this book by testing these methods in their classrooms and to my colleagues, who have read, critiqued and suggested improvements in its format. Thanks to Brian Vince for one of his many poems. And to Marianne, without whom it would never have been finished.

Preface

"We have known for some time that learning (making sense of their experience) is at its best for most children when they are interacting socially and that language and communication is the key to successful learning. 'Children solve practical tasks with the help of their speech as well as with their hands and eyes.' "

– L S Vygotsky, *Thought and Language*

Much research has taken place in the last few decades that shows the power of words in shaping people's worlds However, as with all research, there is a time lag between the discovery of new ideas and relationships and their application in the classroom. A number of books have been written exploring the educational applications of neuro-linguistic programming (NLP) techniques in classrooms, mainly in the area of accelerated learning. However, NLP does have a wider application, because it is a model of human communication and behaviour that comprises three broad elements:

1. Gaining rapport and communicating with another person;
2. Effective ways of gathering information about the mental world of another person;
3. Strategies for promoting behavioural change.

As such it is ideally suited for managing classroom behaviour, especially as it uses both conscious and unconscious ways of relating to and communicating with another person. In particular, it has developed ideas and techniques that will allow you to identify and describe patterns in the verbal and nonverbal behaviour of children. This book explores the NLP ideas relating language to behaviour. Language and communication are the basis of successful learning for children. My belief that the forms of language a teacher uses shape the behaviour and therefore the learning of the children in the classroom prompted this description of the ideas and teaching techniques advocated in this book. Its purpose is to get you a classroom where behaviour supports your children's learning.

Learning in classrooms is mediated by the teacher and this mediation is language-based. This book is about ensuring that the language you use increases your pupils' capacity to learn. Carefully chosen language can actively create the mental images and neurological pathways in the brain of the child to produce the desired learning. I have taken the findings of NLP that can be applied to behaviour and converted them into practical ways of talking and behaving in the classroom.

All experienced teachers have watched or listened to an exchange between a student teacher and a pupil and recognised that turning point in the conversation when conflict becomes inevitable, triggered by the student's inappropriate verbal response to the pupil. I want all teachers to have at their command the widest repertoire of linguistic tools so that they can alter the direction of any exchange with a pupil to move it away from conflict and towards the restoration of a learning climate in the classroom.

In 1994, a UK government circular stated that behavioural problems with children were "often engendered or worsened by the environment, including schools' or teachers' responses". Stop for a moment and remember an exchange with a pupil that didn't go the way you wanted it to. Was your response to the situation as good as it could have been? What did you say that worsened the situation? Now think of being able to communicate with just the right language to get the positive outcome you intended. This is what the NLP language patterns contained in this book can help you to do. The book will show you how to use these patterns in such a way that you will be able to improve the behaviours of the pupils you teach. They are easily learned ways of talking that you can develop into an unconscious competence in your classroom. With your new competence will come reduced levels of tension and noticeable shifts in the climate of the classroom. Just as different colours have been shown to affect mood, so specific language patterns, vocabulary and ways of talking can shift the emotional state of the listener.

Just think of your own internal dialogue in different situations. What do you say to yourself to wind yourself up from a feeling of mild irritation, through annoyance, to full-blown anger? Equally, just recall what you say in your head to calm yourself down or move into a state of feeling pleased with yourself. We each have our own internal dialogues which affect our mood or emotional state. Some of these have been installed in our behaviour for such a long time that we have probably forgotten the experience that first prompted them. More importantly, they act like pre-programmed tapes that begin to run in our mind's ear when some-thing triggers them. These messages in turn generate a behavioural response that can sometimes be dysfunctional when we are dealing with a child's misbehaviour. Recognising your own self-talk tapes from the past and learning to create more appropriate ones is a key emotional-skill development for all teachers.

This book is structured with the reader, and what we know about personal learning, in mind. It falls into four sections appropriate to your learning preference:

Part I covers the bottom right-hand side of the diagram in Figure (i): the *what* of the book, its main ideas and the background research that have led to the development of these techniques. Chapter One contains the ideas and concepts underpinning *neuro-linguistic* programming. It gives a brief history and background to the development of NLP as well as a description of its main tenets and how you can implement them into the classroom. This will give you an overview of the field and allow you to decide which ideas can help you most in your classroom. Although this book focuses on the use of the linguistic devices of NLP, the Bibliography lists those authors who have described how these and other powerful NLP techniques can help you enhance children's learning.

Chapter Two contains recent thinking in brain research applied in the classroom. It is a short wander through some of the key find-ings of the research of the last decade into the brain's structure and functioning, as well as the ideas on the use of specific language in modifying behaviour.

Part II (the top right-hand quadrant) explores *why* you will want to read and learn about these ideas. It surveys some of the current behavioural problems and practices in school. It explores what implications these may have for children's learning and behaviour. Much of this work has yet to be really tried and tested in the class-room. What findings do you think you can use and change your

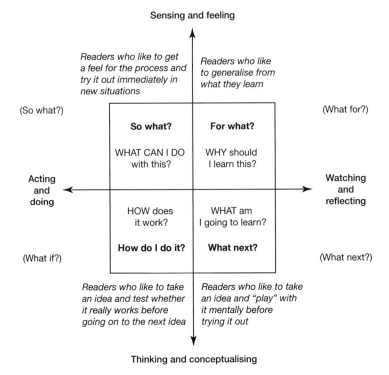

Figure (i): Reading this book

teaching approach? You can be the experimenter and see the effect of some of the ideas in improving children's learning.

Part III covers the bottom left-hand side of the diagram, the *how* of the different techniques and how they are used to gain different goals with the same outcome – better behaviour. This section contains a survey of the words, phrases and scripts of the different NLP approaches to use in the classroom, together with ways of strengthening some of the more common current strategies. Chapter Five has practical examples and conversational "scripts" of the patterns in use. Simply choose a script or a technique and ask yourself if you can remember an occasion when it could have improved the outcome of a confrontation with a pupil.

Part IV concerns *what* you can do with them in different situations. I suggest you choose one or two specific examples from these, linked to familiar scenarios or situations that are likely to occur in your classroom. You can use them when the appropriate occasion arises. Then note the effect they have and consider how the outcome is different from what it might have been like if you had used your usual way of responding. As you become familiar with them, so you can learn others and gradually extend your repertoire of responses.

These ideas can have meaning and worth to you only if you experiment with them in the classroom. An old proverb says that knowledge is only a rumour until it gets into your muscles. In other words, these approaches and scripts have to come *alive*. Only then can you discover and value the ideas and practices described in this book. As teachers, we tend to experiment most with different strategies in the early part of our careers and gradually sort those that have been tested and worked from those that failed. Many of us rely on these tried and tested ways of teaching and then sometimes, unnecessarily, limit our teaching repertoire to them. Under pressure they become our classroom survival strategies, because no one likes to fail too often. Yet "failure" is part and parcel of the normal learning process. Scientists work with the belief that there is no such thing as a failed experiment. Edison always claimed that he did not have a thousand failed attempts to make a light bulb; he just learned a thousand ways how not to make one! Each experiment was a source of feedback on his path to being successful. If, as professionals we shun "failure" by taking no risks, then we run the real risk of forgetting how to learn. In a rapidly changing environment, learning how to learn is the one skill we need most. So communicate well – or disappear in a struggle to maintain a learning environment. In today's classrooms, it is vital to be a good communicator.

Getting the most benefit out of this book

Many teachers ignore potentially useful research findings because they do not value them. They do not value them because they have not experienced them for themselves. It does not matter how rational the research, how erudite the analysis and how persuasive *rationally* the conclusions if you as a teacher have no *emotional* attachment to them, for you will not convert them into practice. Think of smoking: just reading all the research and knowing the likely implications for future ill health doesn't necessarily change the individual smoker's behaviour. Head, heart and hand have to work together to bring about a new behaviour. So, to get the most out of this book, you will need to use the ideas in your classroom. *If nothing is said or done, it remains a book.* You can begin by reading the sections in any order you wish. Read the one that appeals to you most. If you like to see the big picture or feel the need to grasp the whole thing, before you can feel comfortable with practising something new, then read the book as it is written. If you have a stronger, predominantly "suck it and see" approach to your own learning, then begin with Parts II and III. Become familiar with one or two of the actual patterns and use them in the classroom as appropriate situations arise. Note the outcomes and which of these patterns work for you. Continue to extend your knowledge and use of them – they become easier with practice – until one day you will find yourself using all of them smoothly and effortlessly as and when they are needed. Then, if you are curious about just why they have the effects they do, return and read Part I. If you already have some knowledge about NLP you can leap straight to Part IV and choose some of the experiments with the techniques suggested there.

Introduction

"Words are the main currency of our trade."
– Dhority, *The ACT Approach: the use of suggestion for integrative learning*

What makes a good teacher? Why are some teachers really good behaviour managers? When you stop and think about skilful behaviour management in the classroom, what comes to mind? As in all ages and even in this increasingly electronic age, Dhority's words are very true for teachers: words *are* our work! All good teachers are unconsciously skilful in their use of language to engender learning in their students. What changed in the last few decades of the last millennium was the rapid expansion in the scientific knowledge of the brain's functioning and the importance of language in the development of the maturing brain.

The study of how language and action affect the central nervous system is known as neuro-linguistic programming (NLP). Prior to its scientific underpinnings, it was once defined as *an attitude of curiosity that leaves behind it a trail of techniques*. Different researchers followed their curiosity in this field and discovered a range of patterns from which they developed techniques applicable to education. These techniques are finding their way into the classroom and this book takes what NLP tells us about language and communication and applies it to the daily interaction between teachers and pupils.

Many teachers have already found that, by using the suggestions to change their language and their vocabulary, they get better class control through improved behaviour from their pupils. It's not just about talking; it is about developing new patterns of conversation (*ways* of talking) that open up new ways of pupils' thinking. Words trigger internal representations and start processes in our mind. The "right" words are needed to produce the representations we wish to stimulate. We now know that different languages result in differently organised brains.

As the form of the language is different, so the neural paths that are formed while the young child is learning develop differently according to the language being acquired. Learning English, for example, with its alphabet of only 26 abstract symbols arranged linearly to form hundreds of thousands of words, will produce a differently wired brain from that of a Chinese child acquiring its native language constructed of the combination of thousands of individual pictograms. "Language development changes the landscape of the brain radically" (Carter, 1998). Pacific island peoples with no written language develop a wider range of kinaesthetic or nonverbal means of communication. Recent research (Jensen, 1994) shows that even after the language has developed, words can still alter the physical structure of the brain. Brain scans using positron emission tomography (PET) have demonstrated that carefully chosen words can activate the same areas of the brain, and have the same therapeutic effects, as a proprietary drug such as Prozac!

If we extrapolate this research it could support the underpinning premise of this book: altering what you say and the way that you say it can stimulate changes in the behaviour of the listener. As a teacher and a mediator, I believe in the persuasive power of language. This research supports that belief.

Professional mediators recognise three sets of skills in conflict management:

1. Identifying patterns in and behind conflict – patterns in the anxieties that people exhibit; patterns in the individual approaches to conflict as a protagonist.
2. Establishing a climate of nondefensiveness in both parties, which can depend on subskills such as gaining rapport easily, the use of assertive strategies at the appropriate time, the ability to change or modify belief systems and the different ways people see the same facts.
3. Communicating to ensure that conflict prevention and resolution by conversationally redefining positions and issues dampens down the emerging conflict.

This book focuses on the last skill: the development of sophisticated language skills and the linguistic devices and specific speech patterns that ensure improved communication. Although its

Table (i): The NLP language approaches

NLP language type	Types of experience	Purpose or use
Metamodel 	***Sensory & physical*** We experience the world through our five senses, but our linguistic description of our experience tends to be highly selective, with many deletions, distortions and generalisations of the sensory detail of that experience.	The meta-model uses precise questions to recover a fuller behavioural description of the events. It engages the linear or sequential processing of the brain and helps deconstruct the experience.
Milton 	***Conceptual & perceptual*** Whole collections of sensory experiences are generalised and given abstract names such as "love" or "communication", which we then use as if everyone had the same definition of what they mean.	The Milton Model is a form of deliberately vague language to talk to the unconscious mind and to stimulate the brain's intuitive ways of processing to create new meanings or mind sets.
Metaphor 	***Metaphoric & symbolic*** Metaphors and symbols are ways of describing real-life experiences when sensory-based descriptions seem inadequate. Elements in the metaphor, or aspects of the symbol, correspond to elements or aspects of our experience. We use them to extend the meaning of the events they relate to, or to enrich our description of them.	Teachers have always known the power of storytelling to educate and to elicit different emotional states and to promote lateral thinking.

main emphasis is on the language patterns of NLP, it draws on other aspects to aid the first two skill areas. There are three broad fields of language in NLP. They are used deliberately to achieve different outcomes. This book will provide you with a description of the ideas contained in each field, where they can be applied in the classroom and examples of the different speech patterns in all three. Skill in the choice of which mode of language to use and in the specific speech patterns within each field will help create the classroom climate that is conducive to purposeful learning.

Good teachers intuitively use all three ways of communicating when teaching. The aim of this book is to increase your awareness of the greater potential of these approaches when you understand how they can be used deliberately to shape the behaviour of your students. All teachers want to make a difference. Each one of us in education wants to influence for the better the lives of our students. With a greater knowledge of the NLP language patterns, teachers are achieving the positive differences they want, because they understand, first, how the language used shapes the internal world of the listener, and, second, how that drives their outer world, the one of behaviour. And so I wonder how soon it will be before you begin to try out these ideas in a way that will develop the learning behaviour in your classroom.

Part I

What Am I Going to Learn

Chapter One
General Elements of NLP

Having originated some 25 years ago and having developed rapidly over that period, NLP has had an increasing influence on the science and practice of communication. The "technology" of NLP – its conceptual models, its practical methods and techniques – can provide teachers with a wide-ranging understanding of how children think and behave, and therefore how we can help them change. It links what we know about the neurology of our body, mind and senses with our spoken (and unspoken) communication patterns, and helps us to better understand our behaviours. It is based on the knowledge that language does much to determine the development of the neural pathways in our brains and therefore, over time, programs much of our behaviour. This idea of habitual reinforcement of the brain's physiology through language to strengthen some neural connections in preference to others is evidenced by the assertion that, of the 80,000 or so thoughts you may have today, probably at least 60,000 are the same as yesterday's!

The set of processes which have been developed in NLP help you to:

- Develop relational and influencing skills through improved rapport;
- Use easily identifiable language patterns to communicate more powerfully;
- Recognise the motivational patterns of individual children and therefore respond more effectively to their behaviour.

Up to now, in education, NLP has impacted mainly in the field of accelerated learning and not in behaviour management. However, experienced teachers already use a range of the wider basic ideas of NLP in an intuitive way, having developed their own personal classroom strategies through trial and error in the hurly-burly of dealing with the year-on-year task of teaching the children in their own classrooms. Since the 1980s, the ideas and techniques of NLP in improving communication have been applied in projects in teaching and learning (e.g., Jacobsen 1983; Grinder, 1991; Blackerby, 1996). They have been found to be very practical ways of improving children's motivation and therefore their behaviour and their learning. The more you can use the techniques to gain the understanding of the linkage between words and behaviour, to explore your own experience in the classroom and what you do with it, the more you can bring about behavioural change in your students. And your teaching will become more effective.

Remember, all the ideas presented here are *models*. Like all models they are representative of reality, not reality itself. The worth of any model lies in its usefulness in helping us address current problems or issues. Newton's model of gravity is not our current understanding of the mathematics of the universe; it was replaced by Einstein's model because his equations solved problems that Newton's couldn't. However, that does not detract from the huge leaps forward in our understanding of the world that flowed from Newton's model. It helped solve three hundred years' worth of problems. Nor does it alter the fact that it still has application, including the calculations behind first putting a man on the moon's surface! So it is with the NLP models. There is no claim that they are what really happen inside the mind. As with Newton's gravity theory, though, applying the NLP ideas has resulted in remarkable achievements over the last thirty years in the fields of health, therapy and, more recently, education. Now is the time to apply them specifically to behaviour management. You can judge their usefulness.

The NLP mindset: guiding principles for excellent behaviour managers

The current practice of neuro-linguistic programming is based on a set of principles or key beliefs. Success in managing children's behaviour depends on your own attitudes, beliefs and values. They help you to clarify your own values and to notice their effect on your relationships with your students. This set of key beliefs has been selected from the NLP principles most relevant to behaviour management in the classroom. *You may not believe them all, yet;*

for some, just act as if you did believe them. Don't think that you will always find this easy, but you can notice the changes that occur when you can act as if you believe them all. The practices recommended in this book are based on these principles.

1. Behaviour is the best bit of information about a person

Only a fraction of any spoken communication is carried by the actual words. Your tone and other qualities of your voice will carry a message four or five times stronger. All behaviour serves as a communication. Your task is to develop a behavioural "language" that will work in managing pupils. Applying this principle means observing closely what they do, without interpretation, without "mind-reading" – you don't need to know the why of what they are doing. In NLP answering the question *"How* do they do what they do?" is considered far more useful in getting to a win/win state than in seeking a reason for *why* pupils do what they do.

2. People are not their behaviour

Be clear of the conceptual *level* of your thoughts and actions. As a teacher you already take care to describe the child's *behaviours* as not acceptable, not the child's *identity* as a person. This relates to Robert Dilts's neurological levels (see "The levels of meaning").

3. Every behaviour has a positive intention behind it

It may not always seem that way to you, but somewhere, at some level, everyone behaves out of a good intention. It may be hard to see it from your viewpoint. You will have to see it from theirs, to get a feel for what it means to them. But, whatever it seems like to you, their behaviour is intended to be useful to them or to be protective of their wellbeing. William Glasser (1998) in describing his "choice theory" makes the same point slightly differently: "We always choose to do what is most satisfying to us at the time." An important skill in behaviour management is the ability to interpret the underlying message being conveyed by the behaviour and not to focus solely on the behaviour itself. It is good to ask oneself, "What is this behaviour a symptom of?" or "What is the need underlying this behaviour that the student thinks will be met by acting this way?"

4. Emotions are facts

Emotions have to be taken into account in your everyday life. They are real, even if self-generated, and will affect your behaviour. Your emotional feelings are the result of an interaction between what you tell yourself about your experience and your basic gut feelings. So you bring them into existence and, once present, they have to be incorporated into the equation of how you interact with children.

5. There are no difficult children, just difficult relationships and inflexible teachers

"Difficult" children are those children you give up on when you cease to be flexible in your responses to them and communication is broken off. Resistance is not so much an attribute of *them* but more a measure of *your* inflexibility of response. This can be hard to accept, let alone believe, but experiment with behaving as if you did believe it and notice the differences in the responses you get. This book is designed to increase your flexibility by enlarging your repertoire of techniques.

6. The meaning of my communication is the response I get

Many communicators are too busy talking to notice the effect of their message. The surest way to know what you have "said" to another person is to listen to the response you get back. You may know what you meant but, if the response does not confirm that your particular message was received, then you know you didn't convey it – you sent a "missage". They missed your point. You will have to rephrase it until it becomes a message – something they can understand. When a child asks an off-the-wall question, ask yourself, "How is it possible that this child can ask such a question at this moment?" The answer to that question lies in the question asked. What have *you* not done or said that could trigger that particular question in the child's mind?

7. All children have the resources they need to meet the challenges of everyday living

Children are often unable to find within themselves new ways of behaving, because they are in an emotionally unresourceful state. Anxiety distorts behaviour and thinking closes down with high levels of negative emotion. With it goes the ability to find solutions within oneself. Relieving anxiety or reducing its level is the first step in helping a child look for alternative behaviours. This belief in the individual's own innate resourcefulness is an underpinning principle of "brief counselling" approaches.

8. We all have our own internal map of reality

A map is just a symbolic representation, a model, not reality. We create our world by the words we use to describe what our senses tell us. We select from our senses what it is that interests us, and our own past experiences and learning help us decide what we will pay attention to in the world around us, what we will focus on. Two people can look at the same car accident and describe it in two very different ways. Two people can look at the same picture and see two different images. The word pictures we have created in our own mind to describe the picture are just that – in our mind. They are not the original event that prompted them. By the time children have come to you they are likely to have answered three questions for themselves: "What sort of person am I?"; "What sort of world am I in?"; "What happens in a world like mine to someone like me?" The answers to these questions may seem distorted or illogical, but are very real to them; and they will have helped design their internal mental map – their worldview.

9. Children respond to *their* map of the world – not yours

A consequence of the above is that all children do things for *their* reasons, not yours! It makes sense in their unique maps of the world. And that's the world you are going to have to enter to make a genuine difference in their behaviour! You may demand compliance in learning, but, if you do, you are unlikely to get commitment to it!

Some of the key elements of NLP

1. The simple NLP communication model

In *A Brief History of Everything*, Ken Wilber wrote:

> The brain physiologist can know every single thing about my brain – he can hook me up to an EEG machine, he can use PET scans, he can use radioactive tracers, he can map the physiology, determine levels of neurotransmitters – he can know what every atom of my brain is doing, and he still won't know a single thought in my mind … And if he wants to find out what is going on in my mind, there is only one way that he can find out: he must talk to me.

Wilber makes the point that the scientist can know everything about the concrete "exterior" of the mind in terms of the brain and the nervous system, but the "interior" of another's mind can be revealed only through dialogue with that person. It is a black box to us – we see a container and we see the behaviours it produces, but have little idea what is inside the container that results in that observable output. Scientists are well used to dealing with this problem and circumvent it by constructing a model. Indeed, science is a discipline that spends its time devising better and better models of the observable realities that interest it. NLP has a particularly elegant model of human communication (Figure 1.1). The human mind has to be very selective in what it pays attention to, since it receives up to two million pieces of data every second! It has to reduce the complexity of all this information if it is to make sense of what it is experiencing at any one moment. The brain's primary task is to keep the body healthy physically (and psychologically). Perceiving the environment demands selection – choosing just what sensory input to pay attention to – and its prioritisation. We therefore disregard what we consider unimportant at that time.

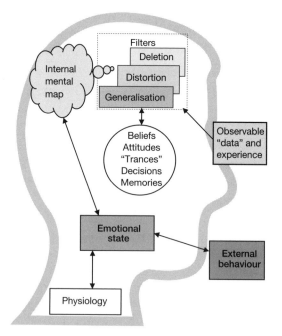

Figure 1.1: The NLP communication model

What we pay attention to depends largely upon our beliefs and values. It is these that help us select the data that fit our mindscape and transfers these as chosen memories for our conscious mind, so that we can easily recall them later on. In the model, these selection and perception processes are represented by the three filters of deletion, distortion and generalisation. (And remember, this is only a model – it is not reality! The idea of filters is only a convenient way of thinking about the internal processes. What they represent is the process by which we choose from all the data surrounding us that which we consider "information". That is, data that mean something to us and will inform our future behaviour and beliefs.)

Apart from the need to cut down the sheer volume of information bombarding us, the main psychological driver for the deletion, distortion and generalisation processes is to shape the incoming information to fit our internally held view of ourselves and the world we inhabit. In this way, we maintain our beliefs, our values and our own self-image.

Chosen data or pieces of information are often associated with an emotion which makes their recall easier. The rest of the unwanted (unwanted, that is, for right now) two million bits of data may be stored below our threshold of conscious awareness. However, your *unconscious* mind notes them and, driven by your deep beliefs and values, may prompt you to behave in a way that does not always seem logical to your consciously aware, thinking mind. John Grinder (1991) puts this slightly differently by asserting that the *literal* part of the message is understood at one level, while its *intent* is absorbed at another. "We know more than we can tell" (the philosopher Michael Polanyi).

This may partly explain Georgi Lozanov's (1979) belief that communication between individuals can take place at more than one level. Specifically, he maintained that all communication impacts on the para- or subconscious mind as well as the conscious mind. More importantly, these two minds could take different meanings from the same surface messages. There is some evidence to suggest that the right and left brain hemispheres are involved in this differentiation. For most people, when they are listening to someone else, the left hemisphere of the frontal lobes of the brain operates sequentially on the words it hears and their specific meaning, while the right seems to work on the tone, volume and context in which the words are spoken. It is therefore more sensitive to hidden messages – the "music behind the words". From his belief in this split-level communication, Lozanov developed his concept and practice of "suggestology" – the skills of *deliberate* multilevel communication. He also used music in a planned way to improve the learning of his students because music engages many areas of the brain in both left and right hemispheres. This helps students learn holistically.

Since then studies have shown that music can play an important part, not only in cognition, but also in the development of emotional intelligence. As Eric Jensen (1994) says, we have "brains built for learning". More and more we are realising the importance of the learning that goes on in an unconscious way – the many learnings that seem to bypass the conscious mind. And, more and more, we are becoming better at communicating with that unconscious mind in a deliberate way to promote learning. As a teacher, you too can develop this skill and greatly improve the management of learning in your classroom. Remember, all learning and creativity takes place in the unconscious mind. Here too lie our memories. They arise from the levels of our unawareness to be expressed by the conscious mind (Figure 1.2). NLP seeks to help improve the communication between these two levels of the mind in order to improve our problem solving in the outer world.

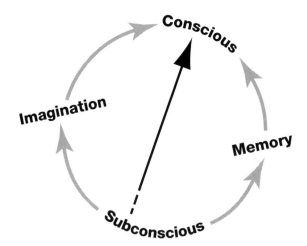

1.2: The conscious–unconscious mind connections

Lozanov (1979) also asserted that a learner's full capability is constrained by the social norms that surround him. This implies that the school's norms can limit the child's beliefs about what is possible for himself and interfere with his growth to full potential. One of the teacher's tasks, then, is to relieve the child's anxieties about any such norms and free him from their constraints. Only then can the full learning potential of the child be realised. Language and the selective use of vocabulary and careful sentence construction can be a powerful aid to reducing anxiety in the listeners.

2. The levels of meaning

Another key concept in NLP is that of "neurological levels". This model was developed by Robert Dilts (1990) to develop ideas about learning and change. As one moves up the levels, more and more of one's personal neurology comes into play. Its application in behaviour management helps you determine what might be the most appropriate and effective level at which to intervene in a particular instance to minimise or change a pupil's undesirable behaviour. It also signals the danger of short-term solutions. These often arise when the problem is addressed at the wrong logical level. Einstein maintained that you cannot solve a problem by thinking at the level that gave rise to the problem; you have to think at a higher logical level. So too with behaviour: it can be addressed at the behavioural level, but its antecedents may be at one or more of the other levels.

For example, does the behaviour spring from a deeply held concept of self at the identity level, or from the child's beliefs and values about herself and the world? Or on her perceived abilities? Or is it really at the behavioural level and dependent on things children can and cannot do? Or is it below this and is a question of just *this* school, *this* classroom, *these* people, *this* equipment and so forth? We sometimes underestimate the influence of the environment on our motivation to learn. Some children prefer a formal setting to a quiet or even silent workspace. There are many such variables and it is always worth checking whether the problem behaviour has a simple root in the environment. The danger of addressing the wrong level is that it treats the symptom, not the cause, and is therefore likely to result in a fresh outbreak at some later date.

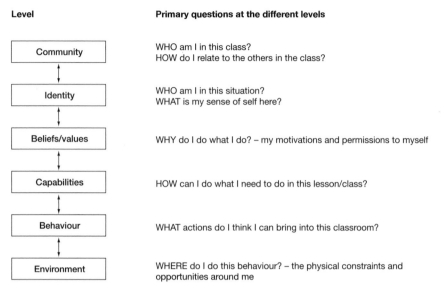

Level	Primary questions at the different levels
Community	WHO am I in this class? HOW do I relate to the others in the class?
Identity	WHO am I in this situation? WHAT is my sense of self here?
Beliefs/values	WHY do I do what I do? – my motivations and permissions to myself
Capabilities	HOW can I do what I need to do in this lesson/class?
Behaviour	WHAT actions do I think I can bring into this classroom?
Environment	WHERE do I do this behaviour? – the physical constraints and opportunities around me

Figure 1.3: The neurological levels (after Dilts)

The model also demonstrates how a simple environmental or behavioural problem can escalate into an long-lasting problem of self-image and then move out to become a social problem. For example, a child stumbling over a piece of classroom arithmetic (a behavioural, or even, on one particular day, an environmental, problem) may, with repeated failure, prompt herself to move up a stage and question her capability at arithmetic. This, over time, hardens into a belief about not just the child's own ability, but generalises up one more level to her identity or self-image – "I'm just thick". After that, returning to the level of behaviour, an individual can forget the steps upward and shrug off the misbehaviour off with "I can't help it: that's how I am, it's just me". This indicates a learned belief about *outcome expectancy* – a belief that what happens to me is outside my control. The belief prompts an internal dialogue of either "It's hopeless" or, worse, "*I'm* hopeless" – an identity response that means I have just degraded my self-image and then justifies my inaction.

Another, related, unhelpful belief is where I think I do have some control over the outcome, but that I won't do very well in achieving it. I have low *self-efficacy* – a belief in my low capacity to learn or to achieve. These beliefs can persist even in the face of contrary evidence. "I may have got the outcome intended, but I was just lucky – I don't really deserve to pass." Roberts Dilts (1990) identifies this unholy trinity of beliefs of hopelessness, helplessness and lack of deservingness as three common barriers to the raising of the learner's self-esteem. They are three beliefs that have to be changed in order to bring the learner's locus of control from outside to inside – to see these beliefs as being at the beginning of the cause–effect chain rather than at the end of it.

It is easy to see how this process moves on, yet again, to a negative disposition towards school and classroom life. If we put the NLP communication model together with the Dilts levels we get what Peter Senge calls "the ladder of inferences" – the process by which many of us create the world we live in, where we consider:

- Our beliefs to be the one truth;
- That these truths are self-evidently true because they are based on our "real" life experiences.

From the NLP communication model, you will realise that the underlying assumption in the above sequence is that the data you have selected from your environment are the real(ly) important data. Once you have made your selection, you can start ascending the ladder and then carry on around the self-perpetuating cycle (see Figure 1.4). This reinforces the sorts of inner dialogue of the last paragraph, when triggered by particular events.

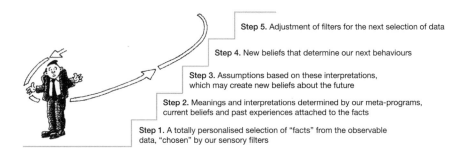

Step 5. Adjustment of filters for the next selection of data

Step 4. New beliefs that determine our next behaviours

Step 3. Assumptions based on these interpretations, which may create new beliefs about the future

Step 2. Meanings and interpretations determined by our meta-programs, current beliefs and past experiences attached to the facts

Step 1. A totally personalised selection of "facts" from the observable data, "chosen" by our sensory filters

Figure 1.4: The ladder of inference

We can all recognise our own triggers, the occasions when someone "presses our button". Once pressed, the buttons start the appropriate self-talk tape designed to raise our own emotional temperature, which then fires the behavioural sequence. The issue for us as teachers is how to break into this vicious cycle of self-destructive behaviours and beliefs and turn it into a virtuous cycle of improving self-esteem.

3. Motivational patterns

As we saw in Figure 1.1, NLP adopts a "black-box" model of the brain – i.e., the brain can be thought of as a complex device within which a number of unknown (because they are unseen) processes work on the data input into it, to produce a set of outputs that you can observe as behaviour. Normally, some of these hidden processes help us to decide what we find motivating and are therefore very significant in shaping our behaviours. The NLP model calls these processes *meta-programs*. We are all familiar with behavioural habits, particularly the behaviour that follows when someone presses one of our "hot" buttons: "I always react like that when someone ... !" These meta-programs are over-arching processes whose outcomes appears as often predictable behaviours. They are predictable because, once triggered, they follow the steps of the ladder of inference. Once you have got to know the pupil, detecting them and utilising them in the relationship between yourself and the child strengthens the degree of rapport and improves the quality of the communication between you.

The meta-programs can be thought of as sorting patterns that run in our brain. At the input end, just what does your mind pay attention to? How does it sort out the huge input of sensory data, thoughts and emotions that it has to deal with continuously? In the darkness of the black box that is your mind, what are the internal processes that work on the inputs, thoughts and emotions and build your internal world map from them? Then, what does your mind pay attention to in what you communicate?

So, the interesting question when we are talking with someone is: what sorting patterns or processes can we detect or infer from his language? Because the very act of expressing his experience or thoughts in a language requires a distillation, a selection of all the words that are at that person's command. It is not a random selection, but one guided by their filters. And what mental operations does this person use in remembering? Preferred ways of thinking are a learned preference – learned in particular contexts. Understanding the contexts helps you understand the person's "psycho-logic". One way of looking at what we term our "personality" is to see it as the sum of our mental mechanisms for coping with life.

Your mind "thinks", or has thoughts, by re-presenting the selected sensory data to itself. When you think of your classroom, your mind may first summon up an image of what it looks like, or replay what it sounds like, or recreate what it feels like – or even how it smells! You may have a preferred way of representing to yourself the classroom and your experiences in it, and a different one (your "lead" system) for accessing that information from your memory store. To make this model useful in transactions between people, Michael Hall and Bob Bodenhamer (1997) classify the meta-programs into five types:

Type I: Thinking drivers – the "mental" meta-programs

We have to learn to sort and pay attention to the incoming data, and so our brains devise ways of processing information cognitively – thus you develop your own thinking style and your own particular "drivers". In practice this means that, as you learn to come to understand your world, you learn to group and sort the incoming data and to make many discriminations and create differences between your experiences. The strategies you develop to make these selections are your mental meta-programs. Some of the important meta-programs related to learning that you can see and hear operating as you pay attention to students working in the classroom are:

i.   **Processing:** Do they deal with new data by either wrapping it up to look at it globally or by breaking it down into its small detail – dealing with the general or the specific?

ii. **Matching or mismatching:** Do they tend to look for sameness and similarity to what they know already, or look for what's new and different, in things that they have not previously encountered?

iii. **Proactive or reactive:** Do they jump into new situations or hang back?

iv. **Motivational direction:** Are they more inclined to move *away* from what they do not like or to move *towards* that which they seek?

v.   **Internally or externally focused:** When they want approval, do they use their own standards or criteria (particularly how they *feel* about something) or seek another person's standards? This is also related to the idea of self-efficacy.

vi. **Working style:** Do they generally prefer (a) to work alone, (b) to work with other people near them or (c) to work collaboratively as part of a group?

vii. **Convincer pattern:** How do they know what they know? Do they have to *see* some evidence, *hear* someone say so or *tell* themselves something? Do they just *feel* when it is so? Or do they just have to *do* it for themselves? How many times do they have to see, hear, feel or do something to believe it?

viii. **Options or procedures:** Children with an *options* meta-program are motivated by the opportunities for new ways of learning and like to experiment, often not waiting for instructions. They want a choice about how they do things. Those who fall into the *procedures* side of this meta-program like to have the security of set ways of doing things and clear step-by-step instructions.

All of these have significance for behaviour management in the classroom, since they can be useful when one is analysing a particular child's unwanted behaviour and when seeking strategies to improve it. For instance, in the first type of meta-program (i), some children will need to see the big picture before being happy to take the first small step towards attaining it, while others will not take that step until the sequence of steps has been explained to them. Children who get impatient when you spend a lot of time spelling out the steps of the task you are setting them are probably right-brain-dominant in their learning approach. They want the overview first – a picture of the woods, not the identification of the types of trees. Those who become anxious when they receive just the picture of the woods are probably left-brain-dominant. They need to know more precisely what is wanted before they enter the wood.

In the second type of meta-program (ii), we can broadly classify the population into four groups – those who:

(a) Look for what matches their mental maps (about 55% of the population in the western hemisphere);
(b) Look primarily for matches, but also recognise mismatches (about 25%);
(c) Look only for the mismatches (5–10%);
(d) Look first for mismatches, then some matches (5–10%).

Matching or mismatching can determine the child's primary orientation towards their preferred style of learning. Schools as organisations tend to be biased towards a matching or "sameness" culture with teachers primarily coming from the first two groups, which might therefore explain their generally conservative approach to change (which by definition is something different!). Children who fall into the first two groups are more likely to succeed at school and become the future teachers, thus promulgating the culture. Children who are in the minority "mismatching" groups are likely to find conforming to a sameness culture problematic and are the ones the conformist culture will tend to label as problems, either behaviourally or in terms of their progression in learning. Therefore, a "matching" teacher is likely to view a "mismatching" pupil as difficult. As learners, mismatchers need time to have the exceptions and different aspects that they notice about the new topic recognised and aired before they get on with the associated tasks. Matchers, on the other hand, need to be able to compare any new material with similar past learning. This gives rise to the idea of "proximal learning" – they learn best when the new topic is close enough to be able to be connected to previous learning, to things that are "nearly the same" as what they already know.

The third type of meta-program (iii) can have a different effect on a child's approach to learning. Bernice McCarthy has devised a classification of learning types (Figure 1.5), in which the proactive child is more likely to prefer the learning approaches of the left-hand side of the diagram, while the reactive child probably approaches new ideas from the right-hand side. The classification uses the two dimensions of how we like to receive information and how we like to process it when we get it. The polarity in each dimension is shown on the diagrams. (The percentages of learners' preferences in each quadrant are the preferred styles for adult learners.) This distinction between how we humans acquire information and how we manipulate it in our minds is vital to an understanding how language can be used to motivate students.

Best education practice says that the knowledge of a child's preferred learning style is the best starting point of any new learning. McCarthy labelled the four learning preferences of each quadrant:

1. **The NFs** – the innovative learners whose main motivation is the making personal sense out of the learning and whose main contributions in a class are likely to be the new and imaginative ideas.
2. **The NTs** – these are the analytical, concept-forming, reflective members of a group. They can never get enough information – the "facts junkies"!
3. **The STs** – the common-sense learners who look for how things work and want a hands-on approach to their learning.
4. **The SFs** – the dynamic learners – those who prefer to find things out for themselves.

McCarthy thought that the ST, SF and NF groups might have a right-hemisphere-dominant approach to learning and the NT group a left-hemisphere dominance. She also links this model with the mental processing preferences, believing that the first three groups would probably learn best through visual material and for the SFs a strong kinaesthetic component, whereas the NTs were more likely to prefer visual and auditory material. You might want to explore whether there is any basis for these connections among your own pupils.

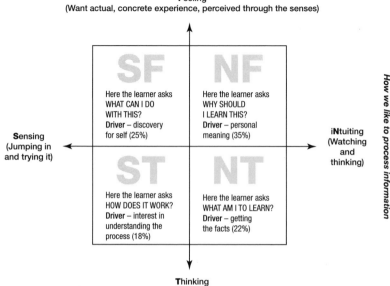

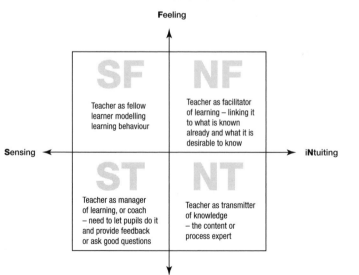

Figure 1.5: McCarthy's 4-MAT

The teacher's longer-term goal is to strengthen the pupil's ability to learn, by developing their use of the other learning styles. Taking the multisensory approach advocated in this book is likely to aid that process and develop the child's flexibility to learn in different modes and therefore respond more positively to the different teaching styles they will encounter in their formal education.

In the fourth type of meta-program (iv), knowing the direction of a child's motivation is an important factor in managing subsequent behaviour. Is she more likely to do what it takes to get what she wants, or do just anything to avoid a consequence? The means of detecting this meta-program is to listen to the language used. For example, you may hear such differences as:

- Towards – people with this meta-program often talk about what they want and describe where they are now in terms of a desired future.
- Away – those who look backwards and tell you a story about how they got to where they are now, starting with what was wrong or uncomfortable for them in the past.

It is sometimes useful to use the simple classification of Figure 1.6 to decide on the next course of action. Children with a towards approach to learning will respond well to clear, positive goals and inducements – a "what's in it for me?" driver. Generally, they will not respond well to negative descriptions of what will happen if they fail. Descriptions of the consequences of not passing the requisite examinations are not the best way of motivating them. However, this may be the best strategy for those who habitually move away from negative consequences as a way of motivating themselves. "You wouldn't want to let graphs spoil your chances of passing the maths test."

The fifth meta-program type (v) concerns how internally focused people make judgments and decisions by checking them out with how they feel or think. How do *you* know you've done well in a lesson? Is it when you feel pleased with yourself? Or when you hear positive things from the pupils and/or colleagues? Or is it when you see the quality of the children's work? Which one of these is most often your initial reaction? Many people look for one of these first and then one of the other two as a backup confirmation.

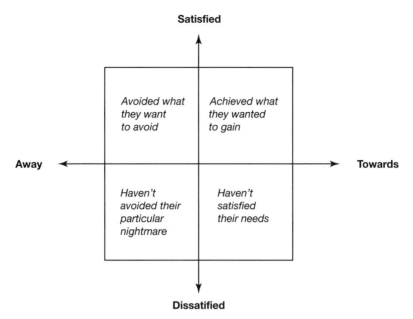

Figure 1.6: The towards/away-motivation meta-program

Children who are predominantly externally oriented will need to get feedback from another person, or see the tangible evidence of the job completed. As you can guess, pupils with an internal preference take less kindly to instructions and are more likely to stick with their own opinion that something is good, even in the face of evidence to the contrary. Allowing them to work on their own ideas is a powerful way to motivate these learners. Those with an external frame of reference want to be told just what to do and are more likely to put more weight on someone else's opinion than their own. Your advice and guidance will motivate them.

We turn now to the sixth type of meta-program (vi). How does the student consider he works best? Does he prefer to work alone, to take sole responsibility for the task? Does he prefer to be left to get on with it, undisturbed by his peers or the teacher? Or does he prefer to work as part of a group, sharing the success and the failure? Or is he somewhere in between, wanting to have clear ownership of a task, but to work on it in the company of others?

The seventh type of meta-program (vii) is important in the reinforcement of learning. The "convincer" criterion for knowing what you know may have to be in your preferred modality ("I'll believe it when I see it"; "I felt it in my bones"). It will also have to be seen, heard, felt, or done, the "right" number of times, or be known for a sufficient length of time.

The eighth type of meta-program (viii) often determines an individual pupil's motivation to begin a task. Children who are options-oriented are often eager to begin something new if they think they have some choice about how the task is to be done, although they may not always show the same motivation to finish it. They talk about what they want, or what they want to achieve, or give an impression that they have a goal in mind. You may hear such words as … I want … I hope that … wish to; I could … I might … it's possible that … if I can just find a way to … I'd … and so forth. Those who are more inclined to the procedures side will be reluctant to begin the task until they are reassured about the steps involved. They often use such phrases as: "What should I do first?"; "I should do it like …"; "I must do it this way"; "I ought to use …"; "I only did it because …"

All eight meta-programs can help determine a working environment for an individual pupil designed to reduce the likelihood of problems. They also demonstrate the complexity of the first prerequisite of teaching and learning, which is setting up a good working environment – one that meets most of the needs of most of the people most of the time!

Type II: The sources of feelings – the emoting meta-programs

 These are what you tell yourself about your data and how you represent them in your mind. We each use sensory or kinaesthetic data and our evaluative emotions to move through life – and we can be confident or insecure about doing just that. Sometimes we follow our gut reactions; sometimes the cognitive programs will dominate and we disregard that feeling. Even within this group, some emotional programs are more powerful than others. Do you know which emotions are drivers for you? In English, we linguistically identify with our emotions – we usually say things like "I *am* angry" (a statement of *identity*). Do you identify yourself with a particular emotion? In helping us handle our emotions it is probably better to stick to a behavioural description such as "I *feel* angry" or even follow the French language and "*have*" anger or joy. That way we would continually remind ourselves that we are not our emotions and that having an emotion is a choice we make internally (even if that choice is often below our conscious awareness). How many times have you heard people say, "I can't help it, it's just the way I am"? They have chosen to accept the internal messages from their past and to use them to predetermine their future. When dealing with your pupils you can help them out of that state of wrongly assumed helplessness by reminding them that they are *not* their behaviour and by giving them permission to be more than their emotions. The skill of choosing "not" to have an emotion is part and parcel of developing emotional intelligence. Many people do this kinaesthetically by "stepping into the other person's shoes" or "seeing it from their viewpoint". Both these tactics usually result in a quietening of our own internal dialogue as we imagine the other person's. William Glasser argues that all our motivation comes from within and that we make the best choices we can to meet our psychological needs. He believes that learning behaviour in the classroom can be improved if students are taught about the "theory" and process of making choices and if classroom achievement was based on cooperative learning.

Type III: The decision makers – volitional (choosing) meta-programs

 These are about choices and decisions. In what direction do you choose to send your thoughts and emotions? How do you run your brain in terms of the systems for deciding/opting/preferring? Choice changes the neurochemistry of the brain. Learning about choices and their consequences has to be an integral part of any behaviour-development programme. Children need to learn that their misbehaviour is a choice they make and that all choices bring consequences, both positive and negative. These meta-programs link the five elements of a behavioural exchange to produce the chosen behaviour:

1. *Awareness* – what you sense

2. *Analytical* – what you think

3. *Emotional* – what you feel

4. *Linguistic* – what you say

5. *Behavioural* – what you do

In times of stress or anxiety, the sequence is often automatic and below the child's threshold of awareness to produce the typical knee-jerk reaction. One part of improving emotional intelligence is to develop the ability to break into the sequence at Step 2 or 3 and not "have" an emotion at a particular time – in other words, to notice your reaction to a trigger and then quieten your habitual response to it; change the rule you made for yourself earlier in your life. What rules do *you* choose to play life by right now? William Glasser advocates teaching children about choices and consequences as part of the development of their emotional intelligence. Such learning helps them take more control of their lives and promotes a more positive approach to problem solving.

Type IV: Knee-jerks and "hot" buttons – responding meta-programs

 Senge's ladder of inference (see Figure 1.4) is a visual metaphor of the brain's tendency to operate recursively: its output from one cycle becomes the input for another. What are your sorting drivers? How well do they serve you socially? Does your own feedback just reinforce your behaviour patterns or weaken them? Most of the rules mentioned above are the results of feedback and decisions made earlier in life. These are often buried in the subconscious but start up like hidden tape recorders to replay an old message. These internal tapes can shape our life and create our future. We usually know our own particular negative messages really well. We may hear them frequently: be perfect, be strong, be on time, be clumsy, don't finish anything, I always lose, nobody really loves me or understands me. They can all produce dysfunctional behaviour in the classroom. We may also have many positive ones: respect others, I am OK as a human being, I can succeed.

If allowed to, all these subliminal messages from our past will determine our behavioural responses to our social experience and our way of being in the world. For instance, in the classroom with other children, will I have a preference for being a team player, a team leader or an independent operator? In communicating with them on a common task, will I most often indulge in blaming the others for the failures I encounter, or always be ready to placate another in times of conflict within the group? All these are ways of responding that are driven by the tapes in our head.

Type V: The dragons in the clouds – the meta-meta-programs

 In Japan, the key decision makers in a large corporation or in politics are not always the visible leaders, the chairmen of the board or the party leaders. They are people who are not very visible but are nonetheless very powerful, well away from the spotlight. They are known as "the dragons in the clouds" – *kumo no ryo*. They may be invisible but their effects are felt out in the world. The meta-meta-programs are the mind's dragons in the clouds. They make up the key set of programs at play in the child's development of undesirable behaviours. They are programs about the previous four sets of programs and they generate the all-important concepts of selfhood.

- Self-esteem   an evaluation of your own *self-worth*. Is it conditional or unconditional for you; is it high or low?
- Self-confidence   an evaluation of your *capability* in a skill. Do you think you can do it? With ease or with difficulty? Is it possible or impossible for you?
- Self-efficacy   an evaluation of your *effectiveness*. How good are you at doing this?

You might want to apply these to yourself in the realm of behaviour management in your classroom. Remember that self-esteem has no concrete existence. It a description of a process – a process that involves adding meaning to what is happening to you, to making judgments about yourself and evaluating yourself. For a teacher this process involves a whole rage of questions such as: How effective am I? How do I rate my own capabilities at handling different children? And how do the answers to these determine my own current self-esteem? When you ask these questions, you are exploring your own meta-programs and can learn about your own thinking. Then, having detected your own thinking patterns from your meta-

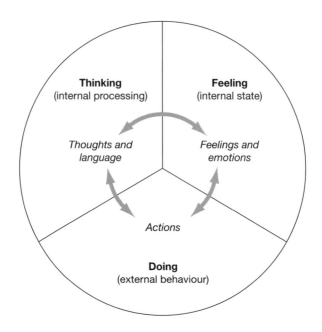

Each of these are interconnected:

- Change your internal thoughts – change your emotions and then your behaviour
- Change how you feel – and what you say to yourself – and how you behave will change
- Change your behaviour – your thoughts and emotions will follow

Figure 1.7: The body-mind connections

programs, you can ask yourself how you feel about the answers to those questions, then how those feelings prompt you to behave, and how that behaviour contributes to resolving the issues you face in your classroom? Thinking, feeling and doing are all linked (see Figure 1.7).

Human beings are hugely self-reflective. However, the danger of this facility is that it sometimes leads us into meta-states of emotion. From an initial state of feeling angry about a child's behaviour, it can be easy to think about that angry response and then, in thinking about it, quickly slide into the meta-state of feeling guilty, or ashamed at having that anger.

Key conclusions

- Fostering good behaviour is rooted in a set of clearly held beliefs about children and their actions.
- Every individual's "internal world" is an interpretation, shaped by what they select from the huge inflow of information coming at them and how they form generalisations about the world from that deleted and distorted data.
- Be aware of the "neurological" or meaning level of any communication between you and the pupil.
- We all have many and varied motivational patterns. You can learn to recognise them through the individual's choice of language.
- All thinking, feeling and behaving are interlinked. Affect any one and you affect the other two.

Exercise 1.1: Know your linguistic meta-program filters

For each of the sentence stems below, tick the ending that best matches you, in dealing with behavioural issues or learning blocks with pupils.

1. The key factor in communicating effectively when managing behaviour is:

   (a) staying in control ❏

   (b) establishing a good relationship with the pupil ❏

   (c) ensuring the pupil gets back on task ❏

2. The way I speak to the pupil in a conflict situation is primarily designed to:

   (a) avoid any further conflict ❏

   (b) establish or maintain a good relationship ❏

   (c) avoid blocks to future learning ❏

   (d) achieve a positive outcome ❏

3. While I'm talking with the pupil it is most important to hold in my head:

   (a) what I want to happen in the future ❏

   (b) what's going on right here and now ❏

   (c) the past behaviour of this pupil ❏

4. When I really want to get an idea across to a pupil, I am likely to:

   (a) paint a picture for them ❏

   (b) explain it logically and rationally ❏

   (c) use metaphorical language or analogies ❏

   (d) engage her heart as well as their brain ❏

5. The key factor in effective communication in difficult situations is:

   (a) being consistent with who I am as a teacher ❏

   (b) staying true to my principles and beliefs ❏

   (c) being able to think the situation through, rationally, to a solution ❏

   (d) what I actually do as I speak ❏

6. For me, I really must communicate well when I don't understand:

   (a) who the pupil is any more ❑

   (b) what they seem to believe or value as important to them ❑

   (c) what's going on in their mind ❑

   (d) just what it is they are actually doing ❑

7. When confronting a child, it is important for me to:

   (a) remember to maintain my position ❑

   (b) get to see things from their point of view ❑

   (c) take a step back and view the situation as a whole ❑

8. In explaining things to a pupil to get past a learning block, I tend to:

   (a) come up out of their specific problem and go to the bigger picture ❑

   (b) give related examples ❑

   (c) break the problem down into small steps for them ❑

9. I know when I'm really communicating well from:

   (a) the sense of satisfaction I get inside ❑

   (b) the reactions of the pupil ❑

   (c) I've achieved my objective ❑

Key to the responses

1. The key factor in communicating effectively when managing behaviour is …

   This indicates your own primary social anxiety when you are dealing with a pupil who is misbehaving and therefore you can better understand what distortions in your own behaviour are likely.

   (a) performance anxiety

   (b) acceptance anxiety

   (c) orientation anxiety

2. The way I speak to the pupil in a conflict situation is primarily designed to ...

   This is an indicator of the away/towards meta-program (mp4) – responses (a) and (c) indicate an away-from tendency and responses (b) and (d) a towards preference.

3. While I'm talking with the pupil it is most important to hold in my head ...

   This indicates your time focus. When dealing with misbehaviour, or when in conflict, are you more likely to deal with the here and now (b), or are you always looking ahead (a)? Or are you more inclined to dwell on what's happened?

4. When I really want to get an idea across to a pupil, I am likely to ...

   An indicator of your preferred sensory modality in explaining:
   (a) visual
   (b) auditory-digital
   (c) auditory
   (d) kinaesthetic

5. The key factor in really effective communication in difficult situations is ...

   Which neurological level is your main driver for yourself in handling conflict?
   (a) identity
   (b) beliefs and values
   (c) capability
   (d) behaviour

6. For me, I really must communicate well, when I don't understand ...

   Which neurological level of the student are you more likely to focus on?
   (a) identity
   (b) beliefs or values
   (c) capability
   (d) behaviour

7. When confronting a child, it is important for me to …

   Which perceptual position are you most likely to adopt in this situation?

   (a) First position (my position)

   (b) Second position (the other person's point of view)

   (c) Third position (someone with an overview of the whole situation)

8. In explaining things to a pupil to get past a learning block, I tend to …

   A pointer to your preferences in the processing meta-program (mp1)

   (a) Big chunk

   (b) "Medium-sized" chunk

   (c) Small chunk

9. I know when I'm really communicating well from …

   This meta-program (mp5) indicates whether you are more internally referenced (a) than externally referenced (b) and (c).

Sources and further reading for this chapter

Blackerby, D A, 1996, *Rediscover the Joy of Learning*, Success Skills, Oklahoma City, OK.

Bodenhamer, B G, and Hall, L M, 1997, *Figuring Out People: Design Engineering with Meta-Programs*, Crown House Publishing, Carmarthen, Wales.

Dilts, R, 1990, *Changing Belief Systems with NLP*, Meta Publications, Capitola, CA.

Glasser, W, 1998, *Choice Theory in the Classroom*, Harper Perennial, New York.

Grinder, M, 1991, *Righting the Educational Conveyor Belt*, Metamorphous Press, Portland, OR.

Jensen, E, 1994, *The Learning Brain*, Turning Point Publishing, San Diego, CA.

Jensen, E, 2000, *Music with the Brain in Mind*, Brain Store Inc, San Diego, CA.

Lozanov, G, 1979, *Suggestology and Outlines of Suggestopedia*, Gordon and Breach Publishers, New York.

McCarthy, B, and Morris, S, 1995, *4-MAT in Action: Sample Units for Grades 7–12*, About Learning Inc, Chicago.

Polyani, M., 1967, *The Tacit Dimension*, Routledge, London.

Senge, P, 1994, *The Fifth Discipline Fieldbook*, Nicholas Brealey Pub, London.

Wilber, K, 2001, *A Brief History of Everything*, Shambhala Publications, Boston.

Chapter Two
Mind your Language!

Patterns of language

NLP has its roots in the study by Richard Bandler and John Grinder of the language patterns of three of the most effective therapists of the 1970s – Milton Erickson, Virginia Satir and Fritz Perls. From these patterns they produced two groups: the first they called the meta-model of language; the second they called the Milton model (after Milton Erickson). The meta-model is a set of questions designed to recover the "missing" parts of a communication and uncover the assumptions implicit in what people are saying. In the formal study of language these assumptions are termed *presuppositions*. The model contains questions that elicit the specific details of an event – usually those that have been extracted by the "filters" illustrated in Figure 1.1: i.e. the information that has been temporarily discarded or altered by the perceptions, beliefs and values of our very personal mind map and generalised by our own interpretations of our life experiences. The use of these questions helps return the abstract words we use in everyday conversation to sensory-specific descriptions of the events being talked about. This results in improved understanding between people.

It is possible to move a conversation in the opposite way from the meta-model, by deliberately generalising it and deliberately leaving out, or distorting, elements of what is being said. This is the Milton model of language, and is a deliberately vague, often ambiguous, open-ended way of speaking, which forces the listener to fill in the missing elements with their own interpretations of what is being talked about. In this way, the listener's conscious, thinking brain is circumnavigated and communication is possible with their unconscious mind.

A third branch of "languaging" patterns employed in NLP is that of "parallel" speaking. That is, not talking directly about an event but telling a story, or providing a metaphor or analogy that contains all

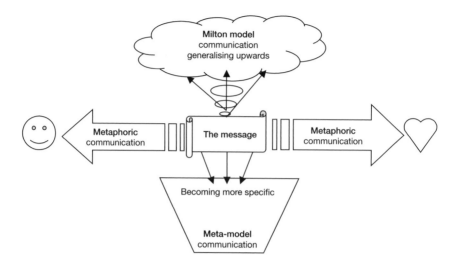

Figure 2.1: The NLP language models

the elements of the event. The story "is a means whereby language and concepts may be developed; multi-cultural and multi-ethnic awareness extended; fears assuaged; hearts touched; and the world comprehended", according to Richard Mills in *Classroom Observation of Primary School Children* (1980). We have all learned by hearing a story that parallels our experiences in the world, and, because it was a story, it was able to bring a whole host of different meanings and associations to bear on our event. Stories can bring new insights to the situation as your mind compares and extends the different facets of the metaphor with the situation you are experiencing. So creative use of metaphor and analogy can be helpful in widening a student's perspective, promoting creative, lateral thinking by breaking the grip of habitual ways of thinking and opening up the possibility of new resourceful ways to tackle an issue. It is particularly powerful in dealing with "difficult" people or situations. All three models are explained further in Chapter Three.

Personally preferred speech patterns

Talking about initial teacher training, Jacobsen (1983) asked, "Are they [teachers] taught to organise information in a way that fits in with the sensory/neurological organisation of the children?" The answer is still, largely, no. However, recent knowledge about the human mind and learning is spreading within the profession. More teachers now appreciate the different learning styles and preferred learning modalities shown in Figure 1.5, which are adopted by children as they grow and develop. More teachers appreciate the tendencies individuals have to use vocabularies based on their preferred mode of learning and preferred way of imagining their worlds. More teachers appreciate that, if they prefer to learn in one particular way, they will probably teach more often in that way. Hopefully, knowing that, they will also then adapt and enlarge their teaching repertoire to encompass all the learning styles in their classroom and use "multiple-representational-systems" talk as they teach.

It is now commonly accepted that every human being learns through all five senses, with some sort of progression over time in terms of the dominant or preferred one:

- Taste (gustatory)
- Smell (olfactory)
- Touch (kinaesthetic)
- Sound (auditory)
- Sight (visual)

Babies have to taste everything – they learn about their world by putting everything in their mouth – so they are predominantly gustatory learners. Taste is closely linked to smell and smell in humans, is one of our least-developed senses, even though, in terms of memory recall, it is *the express train to the brain* – the quickest, surest way of evoking a past experience. (This is partly because olfactory nerves feed directly into the brain's limbic system. It's the closest the brain tissue gets to the outside world!)

When in control of their limbs, children start to learn through touch – they are tactile or kinaesthetic learners. Then they refine their hearing and then their sight. Although we can learn in all these modalities, we tend to have a distinct preference for one or other of them, which can last through adulthood. Schooling is organised to follow the progression of the school-age child. Nursery schools and early-years learning centres are essentially environments designed for kinaesthetic learning, moving towards auditory learners. In infant schools, teaching becomes more auditory in style to match the child's greater responsiveness to the spoken word. At the junior stage the emphasis has shifted to visual teaching as the pupils acquire increasingly better reading proficiency. At secondary school, most teaching is heavily visual and auditory.

The most prized outcomes of the higher reaches of education are those pupils who have transcended the ordinary, representational visual processing to achieve that of abstract visual data handling. The labelling of children who have not switched the dominant modality of their learning at what is deemed the appropriate chronological stage, as having "learning difficulties", is one effect of our formal organisation of teaching and learning progression. That is, a child who is still processing information kinaesthetically when the teacher considers that they should now be a proficient auditory learner is likely to be deemed to have special educational needs. Then, as Michael Grinder (1991) says, such children tend to fall off the "educational conveyor belt". We then employ remedial strategies to try to get them back on that ever-moving belt. Yet some people remain predominantly kinaesthetic learners all their life. That they do so does not mean that they are unintelligent. Usually, it just means that they process information more slowly than auditory learners, who in turn process more slowly than visual learners. We have had the unfortunate tendency in the United Kingdom and elsewhere to equate intelligence with speed of processing, rather than with the *quality* of that processing and its outcomes.

If we accept the idea of preferred modalities, then we need to differentiate between the preferred modality for *acquiring* the data and that of *accessing* it when it has been encoded in our mind. This book is about helping you get inside the individual mindsets of the pupils in your class by listening carefully to the oral output from their mental black boxes. Each child's chosen mode of perceiving or gathering information from the outside world may be different from that chosen to process that information and represent it to herself in her mind. The consequence for teachers is the awareness that some children may have developed only one preferred acquisition mode and have little capacity in the others. Zorba the Greek's preference for acquiring new information kinaesthetically and through metaphor was obvious in his speech in Níkos Kazantzákis's novel:

Zorba scratched his head. "I've got a thick skull boss, I don't grasp these things easily. Ah, if only you could dance all that you've just said, then I'd understand ... Or if you could tell me all that in a story, boss."

Therefore, any information received in these other modes has to be translated into the person's preferred mode. This means that, in teaching a class of thirty children, you will have to teach in at least three languages simultaneously: visual, auditory and kinaesthetic (four, if you include those who prefer to operate audio-digitally.) At the same time you will have to differentiate between the child's preferred information acquisition modality and preferred accessing modality! This links back to McCarthy's 4-MAT dimensions (see Figure 1.5). Some schools have incorporated these ideas into a "brain-based" learning approach to ensure that teachers plan lessons to reach all sensory learning preferences. Putting the learning into the different modalities and telling stories that have the same structure as the learning are powerful ways of reaching those pupils who are not so competent in the learning style assumed by many teachers. The general pupil learning style assumed by the structure of schooling today is that of someone with Gardner's (1983) linguistic and logistic intelligence operating primarily in a visual and/or auditory mode. Teaching to, and for, the other intelligences in a multisensory way is a rarity.

In the 1999 National Advisory Committee on Creative and Cultural Education (NACCCE) report *All Our Futures: creativity, culture and education*, published by the Department for Education and Skills (DfES, previously called the Department for Education and Employment) in the UK, an example is given of a child who was learning through her body. Susie liked writing, but couldn't determine the end of the paper, so wrote past it and onto the desk. Her teacher couldn't get her to change and asked the dance-movement teacher to help:

> Susie moved with lots of "free flow". Her movement seemed to go on and on; if you clapped your hands and said stop it took her a long time to come to some sort of stillness. Together they played "flow" games; letting the energy go, then trying to stop it and hold it inside. Gradually the games moved closer to the skill of stopping at the end of the page ... They got out paper and played, move your arm across the paper and then "stop!" Susie returned to the

classroom and never wrote off the paper again. She needed to learn this through her body, not her intellect.

As Peter Senge (2000) once said, "If your learning isn't in your body, where is it?" – a salutary reminder that all learning is embodied somewhere in our neurology.

Learning from experience

Learning is a natural process. It can be defined by the interaction of our understandings, collected together into a cognitive map, and our key experiences, which give these maps their practical, day-to-day meaning. As events happen to us in the world, we go inwards to our inner mind to interpret them and decide what they mean to us. We then reconfigure our understanding of the world in the light of that event. This is the activity "learning". Learning becomes the connections between my personal cognitive map of the world and my experiences in it. These interactions usually result in the extension of one or other of my two maps. Piaget described the possible outcomes of this process of comparison between these two maps. He labelled them as *assimilation, rejection* and *accommodation* (Richmond, 1970):

Assimilation	The situation is as expected, so no need to change the mental map.
Accommodation	The situation is too different to be rejected, but not similar enough to be assimilated, so our mental map has to be modified.
Rejection	The situation is so different from our expectations that it is rejected and so no change is made in our mental map.

These choices can be seen to be linked to the sameness/difference meta-program described in Chapter One. Vygotsky (1962) came to the same conclusions but described these ideas in a way that gave some guidance to teachers on what new material to select. He suggested that learning was encouraged by offering learners new information or experiences that were different, but close to what was already familiar to them. He described this area of learning with a geographical metaphor, calling it the *zone of proximal development* – the ZPD. This region between our secure space and that of the landscape up to the unknown frontier is often called the *comfort zone*. This varies for each of us over time as we balance the level of perceived threat from the unknown against the amount of risk we are prepared to take. For a teacher, setting proximal goals for a student means describing targets that are challenging but not beyond the limits of the comfort zone.

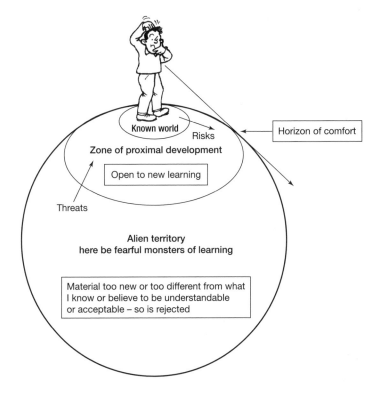

Figure 2.2: The zone of proximal development (ZPD)

Your conscious competence as a teacher is mainly a function of your cognitive map of a particular teaching approach or set of skills. Your *unconscious* competence comes from the types of key experiences related to your skills as you apply them in the classroom. Learning happens when I connect some of my classroom experience to a particular idea on teaching and learning, or when a set of experiences comes together to help form a coherent picture or a new, larger concept. This codification of my experiences around my values and beliefs in my map of understanding is what I can experiment with as I learn new ways of managing children (see Figure 2.3).

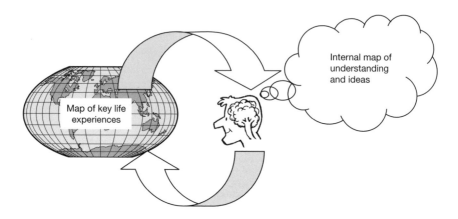

Figure 2.3: Mindscapes of learning

A proficiency in the dance between these two mental maps of experience and understanding is the skill of learning to learn, of gaining metacognition. The data we receive from our environment and these key experiences is coded into our brain's map of understanding in one or more of the following ways:

Sight: Most of us can conjure up pictures in our head of our past experiences and can also imagine future scenarios. We often compare these past and future pictures when trying to come to a decision about a course of action.

Sounds: We can also remember the sounds we hear – these are sometimes stored as words, which we can replay at a later date as self-talk. Such self-talk tapes in the back of our mind can start to play when triggered by some external event and can then dictate our subsequent response to the event.

Feelings: We can create and recreate the full range of emotions, usually by means of those pictures and tapes.

Tastes: Recalling the sensation of taste is so strong we c salivate at just the memory of good food and drink.

Smells: This is the most powerful of the senses in rec experiences, including often long-forgotten memories.

We then code these sensations in our mind through our language. As LeDoux (1999) says, "we categorise and label our experience in linguistic terms and store the experience in ways that can be accessed linguistically". There are exceptions to this, as evidenced by the following extract taken from a posting on the Internet by a Swedish autistic man. He points up the difference between himself and those of us that some autistic people term as "neuro-normals":

An autistic point of view

Autistic people often experience problems with language. They use it in a very concrete and literal way, have difficulties to vary tone and intonation in a normal way, and in some cases (this is probably true for all autistic persons in at least SOME situations) even find it difficult to speak at all. I believe this is caused by a number of things:

The first one has to do with the autistic way of thinking – the autistic mind. It seems normal people to a large extent use words for thinking, sorting out and organising thoughts, feelings, impressions, etc. within themselves. This appears to take place more or less automatically, and the natural state of mind is thinking. This thinking even seems to be difficult to shut down.

Most autistic people don't even think very much in words (however some may do and actually use words to a very large extent and then in a concrete way). For example I think very little in words myself, practically ONLY when I'm communicating (in any way) with others. Otherwise I use pictures, impressions, feelings, or just, experience, things or take in impressions. These impressions are difficult to withstand (like a lot of noise, or many people at the same time). These places then appear overloaded.

There also appears to be a kind of subconscious, more or less, automatic, organising of thoughts and impressions, going on at a very deep level in the autistic mind, where impressions and experiences are put into a context. I experience this state of mind as a different from normal thinking (which I practise nearly exclusively when I communicate with other people) and as more intuitive. It appears to be similar to what normal people call meditation. To meditate, that is, not to think actively, is for me, my normal state of mind. You could say that I don't think, I EXPERIENCE or, take in. Words are also, not really, my native language. I would rather say that pictures, impressions and experiences are.

All this of course plays an important role in the typical autistic difficulties with language. Gestures and expressions of the face are also a great problem to many autistic persons.

When mapping our experience into our brains (Figure 2.4), the different sorts of experience are best encoded in their corresponding representational systems. This is sometimes difficult for people who have a strong preference to code as much of their experiences and learning into one modality. The result is a very imperfect translation – as H G Wells once said, "the forceps of our minds are clumsy things and crush the truth a little in the course of taking hold of it" (Wells, 1905). Men, for example, seem more prone than women to translate much of their primary data not just into sensory-specific language but into a second level of more abstract, non-sensory words (a "digitised" audio modality). Words work for us by reactivating the meanings (and also the emotions) we have associated with our initial experiences.

Sometimes the preferred system is so strong that it affects the physiology and behaviour of the person. Let us look at some common characteristics of people with a strongly favoured representational system.

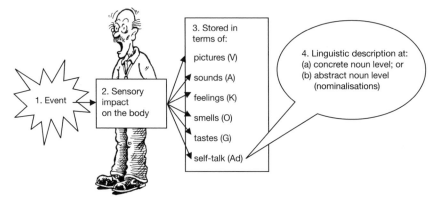

Figure 2.4: The mindscape-making process

Visual

People who have a strong preference for visual processing tend to sit up and forward or stand erect. They breathe high in their chest, which is noticeable by the movement of their ribcage. They memorise by creating pictures and can often be seen looking up because, for them, the answer often is on the ceiling (in their mind's eye)! They can appear forgetful or deliberately difficult because they have trouble remembering verbal instructions. Their speech can be fast, high-pitched and loud. They often have a thin and wiry body and have expansive arm movements, often at upper-chest and shoulder level, or higher. Some of the behaviours that are associated with this type of learner are:

- They remember best what they see and often forget the detail of what they were told;
- They want to read written instructions for themselves rather than have them read to them;
- They may prefer to be an onlooker rather than a participant;
- As they get bored, they start to look around or doodle or stare into space, daydreaming.

Auditory-tonal

Typically, people with this preference, when you talk to them, have eye movements that tend to be side to side rather than up and down. They breathe from the middle of their chest. They learn well by listening and can repeat what you've said quite easily. They like the teaching to be stepped towards the learning goal. They like class discussion and to be told how well they are doing. They may hum, sing or talk to themselves while working. They have well-modulated voice tones.

Auditory-digital

As with the auditory-tonal, the majority of eye movements are side to side. However, they often look beyond you or to the side of you when thinking and talking to you. Their arm and hand movements are small and controlled. Their voice is pitched low and quieter than the first two modes. Both types of auditory learners can be distracted by noisy environments. When bored they may start to talk to others, hum or talk to themselves.

Kinaesthetic

These people often have slow, deliberate speech, with their breathing low down in their abdomen. Hand movements are small and also low, often just around waist level. As learners, they like to be on the move and therefore find sitting still for long periods distracting. They remain motivated best when they are actively involved. They find it more difficult to be an onlooker. So, when bored, they are the people who are likely to be the first to fidget, get up out of their seats or raise their hands to get your attention, for often trivial or off-beam questions.

The perceptual acuity to spot these small differences in a child is a skill worth developing, as it is the first step in beginning to establish strong rapport with the child. Do you recognise children you have taught that fit these descriptions?

War and peace – rapport and disharmony

"The success of my lesson plan has at least as much or more to do with the rapport and atmosphere I am able to foster as with the specific activities planned."

– Dhority, *The ACT Approach: the use of suggestion for integrative learning*

Central to the effectiveness of any teacher is the ability to establish confidence and trust in students. Developing rapport with them enables them to feel you understand them and gives you more information and, indeed, a better understanding of them. Some rapport arises naturally, some you have to create. The skill of getting rapport gives you a greater ability to observe and then get quickly into rapport with the wide variety of children in your classroom. This skill involves accurate observation and behavioural flexibility, both of which require some effort on your part. But, then, you are the teacher. Most of us who have lived long in the classroom consider ourselves able to establish rapport, but part of the process of becoming better at it is identifying how we do so. Learning a subtle skill usually involves unpacking the parts and learning them one by one and then fitting them all together again. Learning here means identifying what you already know, and discovering the rest bit by bit.

Ways of improving rapport

The studies of body language show how people who are getting on well together tend to reflect each other's movements, make similar gestures and adopt similar body postures. As one person changes, the other soon follows. Their mental or conversational harmony is matched by their physiology. This is a two-way process. Achieving behavioural rapport leads to emotional and conversational harmony. Matching gesture and movement of another person is a way of unconsciously establishing rapport with them. It is the process where you adjust your behaviour to be more similar to – and thus in tune with – others. In so doing you are making tacit agreements, which build trust and increase receptiveness and responsiveness. When developing the skill of matching, it is useful to concentrate on matching specific behaviours or other visible "outputs", until you are able to match them automatically and unconsciously. Then it becomes something that you can do – or avoid doing – at will.

Much human communication is conveyed through physiology, including posture, facial expression, physique and breathing. It follows then, that there are some specific outputs that you can match to increase rapport:

- Bodily attitude – upper- and lower-body posture, head tilt, facial expressions
- Key gestures – hand/foot movements.
- Breathing – its rate and depth.
- Vocal characteristics – volume or loudness, pitch, tempo and timbre, which make up the quality of the sound.
- Values – beliefs, principles and preferences expressed during the course of the conversation.

In this way we pay attention not only to the verbal content of communication, but also the "music behind the words". Together with body language, these nonverbal cues can provide essential information beyond the content of what is said. As a lesson in the influence of body posture and position, ask a friend or colleague to undertake Exercise 2.1 with you.

Nonverbal communication is by far the most powerful indicator of feelings and attitude, which is precisely what is often undetectable to autistic people. Rita Carter quotes a person with Asperger's syndrome saying "… people speak with their eyes, don't they? What are they saying?" When practising rapport skills it is helpful to put yourself into an open, receptive state of mind, letting go of your own beliefs and judgments. Then you can:

- Make selective observation of the "outputs" of the other person that you want to match;
- Develop the behavioural flexibility you need to match what you have observed;
- Leave behind your own inappropriate behaviours;
- Seek feedback to check on the effectiveness of the match.

Exercise 2.1: Psycho-geography!

Ask your colleague/friend to remain standing on the same spot and tell her (or him) you are going to ask her the same question from three different positions. Her task is to notice the differences in her response and feelings to the question.

Then, approach her from her left-hand side, stop slightly to the left of her and ask a question such as, "Could you do me a favour and lend me some money?" Give her time to notice and fix her immediate response.

Then move away and approach her from her right-hand side; standing slightly to her right, ask her the same question. Give her some time to notice the differences in her initial feeling and a possible response.

Finally, approach her directly from the front and stop, facing her square on, and ask the question once more. Let her notice her response.

Most people find there are differences in how they react to the question on two levels. Some find they are more receptive to the favour when asked on one side than the other. And some find distinct differences in the emotional reaction to the question in the different positions.

These skills are all important in matching and modelling another person's behaviour. Modelling an aggressive pupil does not mean matching his anger with your anger. It does mean matching the *energy* he puts into his anger. Even with anger, children differentiate between "adult" anger with its degree of control and their own freely expressed emotion. Have you ever been annoyed or irritated with someone, say, when making a complaint about poor service, and become even more angry when they have impassively told you to "stay calm"? We often take this response as a negation of our complaint or of how annoyed we really are. This then irritates us more and increases the likelihood of a further breakdown in communication. Your energy can be displayed at as high a level as theirs (no higher) but expressed as a positive emotion such as concern, interest or willingness to be involved. By initially mood-matching in this way, you are more likely to lead a child towards a calmer state by progressively shifting your energy levels downwards as displayed by a quietening tone, smaller, slower, body movements and other nonverbal responses.

Linguistic harmony

Research with people sending mixed messages shows that, for the listener, only about 7 per cent of the communication is conducted by verbal content. However, this is the focus of most teacher–pupil interaction. The quality of any communication in that vital 7 per cent can be improved greatly by matching the pupil's representational system – using *his* visual, auditory, or kinaesthetic language predicates. Predicates are words that relate to the senses, and most people have a vocabulary biased towards the use of a particular sensory representational system. You can therefore detect that bias in their speech. Table 2.1 contains examples of such speech.

A child may tend to show a preference for one or other of the VAK (visual, auditory, kinaesthetic) systems that becomes more highly developed than the other two and which they will fall back on in times of stress. This is particularly the case when a child is struggling with difficulties in the classroom. They will also have a secondary system, which although not as highly developed as the first, will be used with it in more relaxed surroundings. For most people, the third is usually comparatively poorly developed and therefore they may not seem "tuned into" any information coming at them in this system. So a person whose preferred systems run in the order V-K-A may seem inattentive to verbal instructions; an A-V-K person may seem oblivious of changes in room temperature, or how they are feeling emotionally. Since conflict in the classroom, almost by definition, is a time of stress for both pupil and teacher, the preferred representational systems of both can usually be more easily detected then, than at other times. A teacher who can mentally and emotionally stand back at such times will be able to match the child's language. You can explore your own word use in Exercise 2.3 on page 47.

I have often heard interchanges between a teacher and a pupil who are speaking different languages with both of them wondering why they are not communicating. The teacher says something like, "I just don't know how to get through to her – we're just not on the same wavelength." The problem can lie in the use of different predicate systems:

Mismatching speech predicates

Pupil (K):   "I just can't *grasp* what it is you have to do first with these graphs."
Teacher (V): "Oh, so you can't *see* how they're done?"
Pupil (K):   "No – it seems so much *hassle* just to get an answer to a simple problem."
Teacher (V): "It might help to get the big *picture*, first."
Pupil (K):   "I don't *feel* I'll ever get the *hang* of them."
Teacher (V): "Oh, you will – let's take another *look* at them from a different *angle*."

This pair might have made better progress if the teacher had adjusted her language to match that of her student, as follows.

Matched speech

Pupil (K):   "I just can't *grasp* what it is you have to do first with these graphs."
Teacher (K): "Oh, what do you *feel's* the problem?"
Pupil (K):   "I just can't get the *hang* of them."

Teacher (K): "OK, stay cool, and let's start from *scratch*."
Pupil (K):   "I don't feel I'll ever get a *handle on* them."
Teacher (K): "Well, the first thing you have to *get hold* of is ..."

This may seem stilted to begin with, but making words work more effectively in this way for you is important. When you have learned to pick up and use key predicates in your responses to a student, you will find yourself leading them linguistically to better behaviour. Rapport is strengthened because you are speaking their language.

Conflict and disharmony

A breakdown of rapport (or the failure to establish a high enough level of it) is often the first step in the formation of a conflict between two people. The second is a breakdown in communication between them. Conflict has been defined as "a violation of expectations". Each one of us has experienced disaffection in school at some time, usually when our expectations of the teacher were not matched with the teacher's expectations of us! Often those expectations hinge on perceived competence at a task. Incompetence quickly lowers self-esteem and demotivation turns into disaffection, which surfaces as inappropriate behaviour. Your key task as a teacher managing a difficult pupil may be to manage the misbehaviour indirectly by managing that pupil's expectations! That demands good communication skills.

One classification differentiates between substantive and emotional conflicts. The first are those disagreements that focus on facts, practices, what actually happened – they are primarily cognitive in nature. The second involve anxieties – such as anger, fear, sorrow, resentment, embarrassment – and are primarily affective. The first often results in the generation of the second and sometimes the original focus gets lost in the emotion. Sometimes the conflict has its roots in emotions that generate substantive issues as offshoots of the original anxieties. In the early days of school inspection in the UK by the OFSTED organisation, the effect of the vicious spiral created by the regulator was well known. An imminent inspection first generated a negative emotional response (a range of anxieties), which resulted in diminished classroom performance, which

---

Table 2.1: Predicate words and phrases heard in teacher talk in behaviour management

Visual	Auditory	Kinaesthetic
It appears to me that …	All I hear is …	It feels to me that …
It's clear as day to me	Hey, blabbermouth	Haven't you grasped it yet?
I take a dim view of that	I don't like the sound of that	It feels all wrong
In my mind's eye	Pay attention to what I'm saying	I'm going to lay my cards on the table here
Staring off into space again	Are you tongue-tied?	You're a pain in the neck
See to it now!	In a manner of speaking	Hang on there!
Showing off again	To tell you the truth …	Hold it!
That's short-sighed of you	You've a bell in every tooth	Hold your tongue
In view of your actions	Hold you tongue	Hot-head!
Do we see eye to eye now?	It's clear as a bell to me	That was underhanded
You need a new outlook	Absolutely unheard of	Keep your shirt on
It was plain to see	Yak! Yak! Yak!	Let me put it another way
Look sharp!	State your case	Let's start from scratch
Put me in the picture, here	In other words	My head's spinning
Beyond a shadow of a doubt	Do you hear what I'm saying?	You're a head case
Take a look at yourself	Are you deaf?	Get this straight
Get this clear	I hear what you're saying	Don't push me too far
Let's get an objective view	We're just not on the same wavelength	I'm bending over backwards for you
Can't you see what you …?	You just don't listen	You're a cool one
I just don't see your problem	Empty vessels make the most noise	Don't push your luck
Show me what you mean	Do I have to spell it out for you?	You won't break my heart
Watch my lips		You're just thick
Now see here!		Pull your socks up
Let me draw you a picture		You make me sick
Watch your language		

Some people speak in what is best described as Auditory-digital (A_d) language. Much of their speech is "neutral" with few, or no, sensory words. The nouns are often abstract nouns and the phrases and syntax "computer-like". They use words and phrases such as:

I consider it out of order	I don't think I was
I just know that it was wrong	I didn't do it consciously
I just wasn't thinking at the time	When you think about it …
I can't conceive what was going on in your mind	Rationally, that will …
Professionally speaking	Being objective about it

resulted in poor grades. This has now become a substantive conflict – a "failing" school or teacher.

Avoiding entering the conflict spiral or recovering from the nose-dive in the classroom demands a mix of skills: negotiation and facilitation skills for the first sort of conflict, and the attributes of empathy and congruence for the second. Language is the key in both sets of skills.

Regaining rapport – mediation

When rapport breaks down, you will have to tease out the substantive and/or emotional threads of the conflict. As a teacher, you usually have to be your own mediator. The primary task of a mediator is to open up or to develop communication between two antagonists to achieve a better understanding between them. Mediation is about getting to a future state that is agreeable to both parties. The best mediators hold the belief that the process is all about helping to shape the future relationship between the disputants, not about settling past rights and wrongs. The experienced mediator bases the resolution of an issue on principles of working and good practice, not on positions or power. For a hard-pressed teacher managing the misbehaviour of a pupil, it is often all too easy to fall back on the use of the latter rather than to persist in developing ways of working based on the former.

We also forget about the limitations of linear thinking and look for a ready-made reason for misbehaviour: it's his home, his parents, the last lesson ... Complexity Theory shows us that phenomena "emerge" from the interrelationships between many factors and are unlikely to be the result of a simple cause–effect equation. A useful skill for all teachers is the ability to be in the moment of the confrontation while simultaneously standing back and taking the viewpoint of a third party, a mediator. Obviously, if you can put yourself in the position of the pupil, that helps, too. So you have three points of view: the you, now, fully associated with what's going on and concerned with your own issues as a teacher (first position); imagining yourself in the pupil's position and empathising with *his* issues (second position); and finally the third position – that of the detached observer, the mediator. This is the you who can distinguish between the linear thinking that you might be doing in Position One (that this conflict is located purely in the pupil, and is the effect of some cause or trigger) and the more productive cyclic thinking (that this behaviour is just part of a much bigger system that involves you as the teacher, the pupil's peers and family and the school as an organisation). From this position, new ways forward may arise. Then, with the insights of this observer you, and being guided by them, you may be better able to re-establish a good relationship.

Standing in someone else's shoes is a common enough expression, but not always a well-developed skill. You can practise this triple view of the communication loop between two people in Exercise 2.2 on page 46, and learn to become your own coach to improve your own behaviour management. It will give you an as-if experience of another's point of view and improve your rapport by heightening your awareness of the surrounding geography of the problem.

Another thing to bear in mind is that one of the basic beliefs held by good mediators (see NLP presupposition number 5 in Chapter One, page 5) is that neither of the parties in a conflict is a "difficult" person. Indeed, it is good to hold the belief that there is no such creature as a "difficult person". What there is, for now, between the two people is a difficult relationship. A second thing to remember is that I can change no one – I personally find it difficult enough to change myself! However, if you can imagine a relationship with another person as a rope, comfortably taut, that joins you and the other person together, then you can picture conflict as a time when the tension in the rope is uncomfortably tight or slack. You can ask yourself what you are doing to maintain that degree of tension. What is your part in sustaining the conflict? Then, if you change at your end, the tension in the relationship will change and this might prompt the person at the other end to adjust their behaviour to suit the new conditions.

This concept of the difficult relationship helps peacemakers by directing their attention to the space between the two protagonists. Considering the rope in the gap between them as problematic keeps the mediator away from ascribing problems to personalities and keeps the focus on principles and outcomes. It moves the focus of the conversations from blaming to finding positive intentions. So a good set of questions for yourself as a teacher, facing a child is:

- How am I contributing to this child's behaviour?
- How am I sustaining this difficult relationship?
- What am I gaining by maintaining it as it is?

A good exercise is then to imagine yourself as the child and ask yourself, as the child, the same three questions. We all know the benefits of feeling what it's like to stand in another's shoes. To get their viewpoint and listen to what you sound like from their position. This is one way of breaking unhelpful cycles of your own behaviour patterns.

"What makes this pupil tick?" – strategies in NLP

The term "strategy" in NLP has a specific meaning. It refers to the decision-making process that goes on unconsciously in everyone's mind that results in an outwardly visible behaviour. More than that, an unconscious strategy will produce a consistent outcome from the same starting point, as the steps in the strategy remain constant. These strategies have been derived from our responses to how we perceive the world and what we have decided is the best way to survive in it. We therefore have a strategy for everything we do – from buying a pair of new shoes to falling in love! The strategies we have can be easily learned or modified, depending on the desired outcome. Eliciting the strategy a child uses to motivate herself to do some classwork is a useful skill for a teacher to possess, in order that it can be improved or altered in a productive way.

Strategies consist of a sequence of internal and external processes designed to produce a behaviour. We are usually unaware of the intervening steps we take between the triggering event and the final behaviour – they are below our threshold of conscious awareness. Such steps may encompass all of the different representational systems, but the last step in all decision-making boils down to the person answering one of the following four basic questions to his own satisfaction:

- Does it look right? (a visual (V) strategy)
- Does it sound right? (an auditory (A) strategy)

- Does it feel right? (a kinaesthetic (K) strategy)
- Does it make sense? (an auditory-digital (A_d) strategy)

I once observed a teacher working with a child in her Year 4 class. The child had a history of periodically running out of the room to stand in the middle of the school field. The teacher, knowing some NLP techniques, asked him the disarmingly simple question, "Peter, when do you know it's the right time to run out of the room?" The reply was swift and simple: "When you give me my work, I look at it and if I think it's too hard then I get angry and run out." This told the teacher some, if not all, of the steps in the strategy that led to his decision to run out:

- "... I look at it ..." (a visual external step – V_e)
- "... and if I think it's too hard ..." (the boy telling himself something, an internal auditory dialogue – A_d)
- "... I get angry." (an internal kinaesthetic check – K_i)

So the strategy is:

$$\text{Trigger} \longrightarrow V_e \longrightarrow A_d \longrightarrow K_i \longrightarrow \text{action}$$

This is a fairly standard strategy sequence and, with no formal knowledge of NLP, this teacher now had some idea of how to close down the unwanted behaviour. When she gave Peter some work, she could ask him, "Does this *look* too hard for you?" and, if she got the answer "yes", give him some additional help. Or she could say, "The moment you first feel angry, come and ask me for help" to offer him an alternative action at the point of anger. With an understanding of the linguistic patterns of NLP she could close down the strategy by saying something like, "Look at today's work. It's easier than you think and you can know how good you'll feel when it's finished." It is difficult to stop or suppress a negative internal dialogue. The teacher has intuitively hit on the best way of countering it by offering a positive affirmation instead.

Knowing what you now know about mental meta-programs you might, through other observations of Peter's behaviour, have concluded that he operates mostly from an away-from meta-program. You could improve and strengthen the dialogue even further, by making the last piece congruent with that knowledge: "I'm wondering if you can look [V_e] at today's work and tell yourself that it's easier than you think [A_d] and you can know now you won't feel bad [K_i] at the end of the lesson." This assumes that not wanting the bad feeling of anger is a stronger motivator for him than wanting an unspecified good one. The added power of this communication is that it is presented in the same order and sequence as Peter's strategy steps.

There is likely to have been one step missed out in the boy's description in the process of how he decides to run out. He must have done some other thing in his mind after looking at the work, to prompt the negative internal dialogue. In many cases this second step is a comparison one. Since he said he looked at the work, he may have compared it with a memory of how some past piece of work that he found too difficult to do looked to him. That is, he did a visual comparison of the present work with a recalled picture (V_r) of past work. This might then have prompted the internal dialogue and stirred up again the associated bad feeling of that previous occasion. So the fuller strategy might well have been:

$$\text{Trigger} \longrightarrow V_e \longrightarrow V_r \longrightarrow A_d \longrightarrow K_i \longrightarrow \text{action}$$

Good questioning and observation over time would find this out. The teacher could have asked, "After you looked at the work I'd given you, what happened next that helped you feel angry?" Or, "… what else did you do to …?" These questions might have uncovered additional steps. Such strategy steps are often accompanied by well-established patterns of eye movements. Eye movements indicate how the strategy has been encoded in Peter's brain and the sensory modalities being used in each step. Tracking eye movements is not always easy, since there may be a very rapid sequence of small movements. Questioning the pupil as in the example above helps slow the process down and aids the identification of the discrete stages. As he described his strategy, Peter's eyes might have been noticed to move in the sequence shown in Figure 2.5 (if he was right-handed).

Many motivation strategies fall into these two groups that contain the elements of a visual picture of the finished task with associated good feelings, or a picture of the consequences of not completing the task and its negative feelings. In school learning, an away-from (possible sanctions) type of strategy is often not a strong enough motivator to do the work. A mix of both motivational language approaches is needed: "Look at today's work. It's easier than you think and you can know you won't feel bad at the end of the lesson and you can be pleased with yourself when you leave at break time."

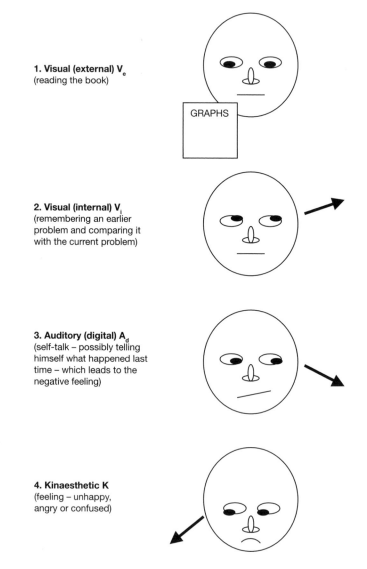

1. Visual (external) V_e
(reading the book)

GRAPHS

2. Visual (internal) V_i
(remembering an earlier problem and comparing it with the current problem)

3. Auditory (digital) A_d
(self-talk – possibly telling himself what happened last time – which leads to the negative feeling)

4. Kinaesthetic K
(feeling – unhappy, angry or confused)

5. Decides to run out of the classroom

Figure 2.5: Peter's strategy

Good decision makers aren't necessarily those who use the more "sensible" approach of the audio-digital. Indeed, good decision makers, whatever the strategy steps that bring them to their decision, often tend to do an internal kinaesthetic check as the final decider – how the decision "feels" to them. This is in accord with what we know about the brain's functioning. It was established early in the last century that "rational" decision making is intimately involved with the limbic system, the seat of our emotions. Rita Carter describes a famous case of a railway worker, Phineas Gage, who in 1848 suffered severe brain damage in which his limbic system was damaged. All other brain functions seemed unimpaired and he lived for many years after, but could not hold down a job, because although his thinking seemed clear enough, his decision making was very poor. He was unable to make that last kinaesthetic check on the quality of his reasoned decision making.

Language is the key to knowing which type of decision maker any child is. The clues lie in the predicates the child uses – the sensory-linked verbs, adverbs and adjectives. So helping most people to change their minds about something really means changing the representation they have of the events in their minds – their pictures of themselves, what the voices in their heads say, or how they feel about them. Only for the small number of A_d decision makers is a logical explanation an acceptable way to promote change. Yet that is the strategy teachers very often use – we feel we must give a reasoned explanation. Such an approach is even less effective when the change sought is in the emotionally charged climate of misbehaviour. You are more likely to influence the other person when you are on her wavelength, talking *her* language. That is, when your choice of vocabulary matches hers, whether it's primarily visual, auditory or kinaesthetic. Then you have the gift of tongues and are able to match the map in the other person's mind.

It is what happens in the third step of the mindscape-making process (Figure 2.4) that provides the key to good decision making. Children who have a preference to A_d will focus their attention on this part of the third step rather than cross-checking with their feelings (the K part), with a reduction in the efficacy of their decisions. They may say, "It just doesn't make sense" as a response to a learning difficulty. If that then links back to a negative feeling, demotivation sets in. Some children have very short strategies involving only two elements. Have you ever heard someone say, "I'll see how I feel about it" when you have asked them for a decision? This is a clue that their strategy in this case is based on a V and a K component so closely connected that one or other may be beyond their conscious awareness. This telescoping of steps is known as a *synaesthesia*. Such quick-fire strategies can lead people to make bad decisions time and time again – they seem to learn nothing from the bad outcomes of previous runs through the strategy. Imagine having a strategy for buying a car that consists only of the V/K synaesthesia: I see it/I feel I want it and *therefore* I decide to buy it.

Perhaps it was just this strategy that led Elvis Presley to buy twenty Cadillacs in one day!

Exercise 2.2: Being your own mediator – a perceptual-positions exercise

This is an exercise that utilises your visual, auditory and kinaesthetic senses and so needs sufficient space in which to move around.

Think of a situation that is live for you now and that is not as good as it needs to be – one in which you would like to improve your relationship with the other person. This could be a pupil, or another colleague, or a member of your family.

1. Choose a position in the room to place a sheet of paper down on the ground and then stand on it. This is your **First Position**. And represents the true "here and now" for you. Think about yourself, the other person and the issue.

    Notice what you can see in your mind's eye, what you can hear and how you feel inside.

2. Look across to another position in the room and imagine that both you and the other person are sitting facing each other there. When you are in this situation you are in a **Second Position**.

    How are those two people relating to each other from this position?

    Step off the sheet of paper and let go of the first position by shaking your arms and body.

3. Take two more sheets of paper and place them in the Second Position to represent the chairs for the two people (say A and B). When you are ready step onto the sheet that represents **Second**

Position A. Take a little time and experience being **A**. Look at **B** from this position … and then back to yourself at First Position.

Ask yourself, What is important to me, A, here in this position? What is not being really dealt with here?

Step off the sheet of paper and let go of Second Position A by shaking your arms and body again.

4. Step onto the sheet that is **Second Position B**. Take a little time and experience/imagine being B this time. Look at A from this position … and then back to yourself at First Position.

Ask yourself, What is important to me, **B**, here in this position? What is not being really dealt with here?

Step off the sheet of paper and let go of Second Position B by shaking your arms and body.

5. Now find another place in the room with a wider perspective, from which you can see all three pieces of paper. This is **Third Position** – step into it.

Ask yourself, What do I notice about the relationship and interactions between the others? What resources are needed here to change things? What could I bring to the situation? What do I notice now that I didn't notice before?

Take the answers with you and walk back to First Position. Step onto the sheet and from this First Position, with all this new information and new resources, take a look at the two people at **A** and **B**.

Notice what has changed, anything that is different.

Exercise 2.3: What is your preferred vocabulary?

Complete both parts of this exercise in 5 minutes or less!

Part 1

Select the group of words that comes easiest to you, from each of the following sets of three – just go with your first impression:

Responses to Part 1

1. (a) perceive, look, see
    (b) listen, talk, conversation
    (c) feel, grasp, touch   a)   b)   c)

2. (a) shake, sensation, hold
    (b) scene, perspective, focus
    (c) discuss, comment, criticise   a)   b)   c)

3. (a) whisper, speak, shout
    (b) handle, smooth, rough
    (c) show, view, peer   a)   b)   c)

4. (a) focus, outlook, bright
    (b) articulate, fluent, silent
    (c) grip, hold, move   a)   b)   c)

5. (a) ring, quiet, hum
    (b) illusion, picture, mirror
    (c) excite, rush, crawl   a)   b)   c)

6. (a) colour, glow, hue
    (b) hot, pleasant, comfortable
    (c) listen, hearsay, rumour   a)   b)   c)

Now select the statement that is easiest for you to read, from each of the following sets of three statements – once again, just go with your first impression:

Selection 1

(a) If I don't hear the bell, the sound of voices in the corridor lets me know the lesson is over.

(b) From my classroom, I can see the brightly coloured toys of the nursery school play space.

(c) On hot days, I love the feel of the breeze that comes through my open windows.

Selection 2

(a) When I teach, I like to feel comfortable. My room must not be too warm or too cold if I am to feel alert and on top of things.

(b) One of my pupils often talks quietly to herself as she works, and, as I listen, I can hear myself as a young child, saying the same sorts of thing.

(c) I like to gaze through the windows and watch the scene outside – that's when I think best.

Selection 3

(a) The new students appeared surprised at what they saw in my room. Their pleasure was visible in their faces.

(b) Walking about the room as I teach, I get a better feel for what everyone is doing. My legs can get tired by the end of the day and I like to stretch them when I am relaxed at home.

(c) Children will usually say a lot when you talk about their interests. They get verbally animated and become more fluent.

Selection 4

(a) Creative children see patterns and colours that others just do not notice. They can paint interesting pictures from the sight of quite mundane objects.

(b) At the sound of the first instrument, my students pricked up their ears. When the full band came in, the tempo and rhythm soon had them humming or singing.

(c) The touch-box lesson provided so many different sensations that I could myself feel the range of emotions produced by the children – from pleasure at the furry object to disgust at the cold, slimy ones.

Selection 5

(a) Communicating effectively when teaching means giving students feedback that they can hear. That means being in tune with them and their learning concerns.

(b) I like to understand the learning anxiety of a specific child. I feel that I can then create an environment for her in which she feels secure and happy to learn.

(c) Children watch teachers all the time. They model their responses on what they see adults doing.

Part 2

Circle the expression that comes easiest to you in each of the triple choices:

1. (a) they're hand in hand
   (b) we don't see eye to eye
   (c) he copied me word for word   a)   b)   c)

2. (a) did you get and an eyeful
   (b) I gave him an earful
   (c) he's a handful   a)   b)   c)

3. (a) do you hear what I'm saying?
   (b) do you get the picture?
   (c) do you feel OK with that?   a)   b)   c)

4. (a) you've had a sudden flash of inspiration?
   (b) are any bells ringing now?
   (c) do you feel you're close to a solution?   a)   b)   c)

5. (a) hang on in there
   (b) you can rise above this
   (c) look at it from my point of view   a)   b)   c)

6. (a) that behaviour is short-sighted of you
   (b) that behaviour is underhand
   (c) that behaviour speaks volumes   a)   b)   c)

Scoring sheet

Circle your response for each item and then total the three columns:

Part 1

Q. 1	a)	b)	c)
Q. 2	b)	c)	a)
Q. 3	c)	a)	b)
Q. 4	a)	b)	c)
Q. 5	b)	a)	c)
Q. 6	a)	c)	b)
Selection 1	b)	a)	c)
Selection 2	c)	b)	a)
Selection 3	a)	c)	b)
Selection 4	a)	b)	c)
Selection 5	c)	a)	b)

Part 2

Q. 1	b)	c)	a)
Q. 2	a)	b)	c)
Q. 3	b)	a)	c)
Q. 4	a)	b)	c)
Q. 5	c)	a)	b)
Q. 6	a)	b)	c)

Total   _____   _____   _____

Column 1 represents your total VISUAL score

Column 2 presents your total AUDITORY score

Column 3 represents your total KINAESTHETIC score

Do you have a markedly preferred mode? Your highest score may denote the primary mode you use in communicating with the people around you and is likely to be the one you use most in dealing with conflict. Your second highest will probably be used frequently in everyday conversation alongside your first preference. The lowest score is the one you are likely to use least and therefore may be the one that you are particularly insensitive to. Under conditions of stress most people fall back on their preferred modality.

Key conclusions

- Each of us shows a bias towards a particular vocabulary usually based on one or other of our senses of vision, hearing or feeling.
- Most people take "calculated risks" when learning: they will move only so far out of their comfort zone so that we can link the new learning to an already familiar experience.
- Greater rapport with pupils and mutual understanding can be gained by speaking to them using their own preferred sensory vocabulary.
- We all have many and varied decision-making patterns that lie behind our choice of observable behaviour. You can learn to recognise them through the individual's choice of language and the observation of eye movements.

Sources and further reading for this chapter

Carter, R, 1998, *Mapping the Mind*, Weidenfield and Nicolson, London.

Dhority, L, 1991, *The ACT Approach: The Use of Suggestion for Integrative Learning*, Gordon and Breach Science Publishers, SA.

Gardner, H, 1983, *Frames of Mind: The Theory of Multiple Intelligences*, Basic Books, New York.

Grinder, M, 1991, *Righting the Educational Conveyor Belt*, Metamorphous Press, Portland, OR.

Jacobsen, S, 1983, *Meta-Cation: prescriptions for some ailing educational processes*, Meta Publications, Cupertino, CA.

Le Doux, J, 1999, *The Emotional Brain*, Phoenix, London.

Mills, R W, 1980, *Classroom Observation of Primary School Children*, Unwin Education Books, London.

National Advisory Committee on Creative and Cultural Education (NAC-CCE), 1999, *All Our Futures: creativity, culture and education*, National Advisory Committee on Creative and Cultural Education, a Department for Education and Skills publication, Sudbury, Suffolk.

Richmond, P, 1970, *An Introduction to Piaget*, Routledge & Kegan Paul, London.

Senge, P et al., 2000, *Schools That Learn*, Nicholas Brealey, London.

Vygotsky, L S, 1962, *Thought and Language*, MIT Press, Cambridge, MA.

Wells, H G, 1905, cited in Koestler, 1970, *The Act of Creation*, Pan, London.

Part II

Why Should I Learn This?

Chapter Three
What's Happening in Classrooms Now?

"If children come to feel that the universe does not make sense, it may be because the language we use to talk about it doesn't make sense."

– John Holt, *How Children Fail*

Establishing a peaceful classroom for learning is the goal of all teachers. *Maintaining* a peaceful classroom now demands a complex set of skills, since it has become an increasingly difficult task over the last decade. Everyone working in education agrees that the pressures on teachers have never been so intense. Pressures come in the form of having to demonstrate competence to practice, of having to achieve targets for pupil attainment, of having to satisfy the demands of parents and of accountability through external inspection. Such pressures can promote behaviours that work against the maintenance of good teacher–pupil relationships in the classroom. When the delicate balance between task accomplishment and relationship is wrong, misbehaviour follows on.

In 2001, in the light of the emergence of a global digital communication system, Professor Stephen Heppel raised the question of whether we could continue to teach a nationally defined curriculum, using the same methods as we currently do. The technologies behind a global network could be harnessed to provide more flexible ways of learning, more individually tailored, student-centred programmes that would harness and build on individual creativity. Currently, British schools are controlled by a national agenda with its emphasis on standardisation and targets, which has resulted in a lack of professional confidence. The changes brought about by changing technology demand a flexible teacher population to respond to the different pedagogy. And flexibility is a casualty of low professional confidence. The growth of the global digital communication network is already providing an alternative to traditional schooling. It is beginning to provide a draw for excluded pupils and the school refusers. For now, however, until such alternative learning becomes a reality for all students, teachers will still have to provide a learning environment for the disruptive and the disaffected. However, the picture is not all dark. Over the last decade or so, a lot of excellent advances supporting the development and maintenance of productive learning behaviour have come out of the different fields of:

- The management of behaviour;
- The psychology of behaviour;
- Brain functioning and learning;
- Neuro-linguistic programming (NLP).

Since this book is about this last field, this chapter skims lightly over the relevant developments in learning behaviours that relate to NLP practice in the other three fields, just to provide a context for the learning of its new language skills.

Managing behaviour

Louise Porter has classified the theories and practices of behaviour management evident in current use in our schools and she has placed them on a spectrum dependent on their underpinning belief systems and rationales. They stretch broadly from more authoritarian approaches through to more liberal mindsets. They can also be aligned with the neurological-levels diagram (Figure 1.3). Teachers often use an eclectic mix of the techniques that fall out of these different theoretical approaches. For most teachers, they are not usually based on a conscious choice between the different approaches, but on the tried and tested principle of pragmatism – on what has worked in the past! However, heading the list of what *children* say is that what good teachers do to get everyone in the class working well, without disruption, are:

- They take time to explain and help with problems without making the pupil feel silly or look foolish in front of peers;
- They have a positive relationship with the pupils, being willing to laugh and joke with them while showing that they are genuinely interested in them;

- They communicate clearly the operating rules of the classroom and are fair in applying what sanctions have been agreed for when those rules are broken.

This research confirms what good teachers know instinctively: good relationships and clear communications are the keys to opening up the classroom as a learning place. Good planning and clear systems for agreeing class routines and rules, with purposeful behavioural goals appropriately negotiated, *maintain* it as a learning place. Under the pressures of a wayward group of pupils, it is easy to lose sight of the fact that behaviour management systems are means to a learning end and not ends in themselves.

Many schools still operate behaviour-management systems that incorporate different forms of rewards and sanctions even though much research demonstrates their limited benefits. This is mainly because such systems are an attempt to motivate pupils *externally* rather than to create a system that encourages and develops self-motivation – motivation that is *internally* driven. These internally driven systems create environments that promote the American humanistic psychologist Abraham Maslow's self-actualisation ideals (this is the term Maslow applied to the fulfilment of one's greatest human potential). It is now commonly found that reward systems decrease creativity and that the quality of learning is poorer than that which takes place in other systems. One reason for this is that it tends to shift a teacher's energy into being a classroom monitor, rather than being the classroom's manager of learning.

Another reason may be that the introduction of such a system, of itself, raises anxiety levels and negative emotions within the classroom. Indeed, the research goes further and asserts that reward systems actively sustain low levels of achievement. An NLP saying is, "Energy flows where the attention goes." That is, if you focus on something like punishment, then you will spend much time punishing. This encourages children to learn the "pay-off principle" – learning to do only what is necessary to gain the rewards and avoid the punishments – even if the punishments are merely the withdrawal of the rewards. Children quickly learn that schooling is about "playing the game", which is hardly a healthy mental attitude for positive lifelong learning. More frightening is that this is the very principle that a generation of British teachers themselves

Table 3.1:   Classification of behaviour-management approaches

Underpinning approach	Louise Porter's classification	Logical level
Behaviour theory	1. Limit-setting approaches – based on the teacher's right to impose order and to discipline those who break the rules (e.g., "assertiveness discipline")	Environment
	2. Applied behaviour analysis – based on the ideas of behaviour modification, including reinforcement of positive behaviour and "punishment" of undesirable behaviour	Behaviour
Mix	3. Cognitive-behaviourism – behaviour-modification approaches incorporating the student's thinking processes to promote self-discipline and to move away from externally imposed systems to regulate behaviour	
Cognitive	4. Neo-Adlerian – such as the STET approach (Systematic Training for Effective Teaching) based on developing cooperative relationships	Capability
	5. Choice theory – an approach utilising the ideas of both Types 3 and 6, based on the belief that all behaviour is (consciously or unconsciously) chosen, and chosen to meet a need	Beliefs & Values
Pupil-centred approaches	6. Humanistic/"democratic" relationships between teachers and students aimed at meeting their emotional needs and nurturing their innate curiosity for learning	Identity
Systems theory	7. Systems theory – this is based on behaviour as a result of the interactions between the complex sets of relationships that exist in any organisational system; despite it being complex, it is possible to see patterns in such systems and to derive laws about them	Community

have learned in developing an educational system that focuses on school targets that are nationally inspected. Such inspections can result in a distribution of OFSTED rewards (positive reports) and sanctions labelled "in need of special measures", "failing" etc. Teachers will play the game to avoid these last categories. And children model teachers!

Adam X

My name is Adam X
It used to be Adam Walsh
But every time I see my name
It says Adam X

My mate's Martin Smith
He's now Martin X
Yesterday he was Martin XX
Today he's Martin X again.
We ain't related.
We never met until he came here
to this school and my class.
But now we must be brothers.
We must be.
We've got the same name

I was Adam Walsh
until I tapped my pencil
The teacher said
"Stop tapping your pencil Adam"
And I did

Then I'm thinking again
and my pencil taps,
almost on its own.
"Adam. I warned you
I'll write your name on the board"
He did

And I was just Adam.

There it goes again,
as I think about
the really exciting bit
of my story

Tap.

"ADAM!"
and Adam X was born.

Happens a lot now
I don't mind.
I got lots of family now.
Keith and
Stuart and
Kylie and
Sam and
Martin of course
We're all "eXis"

I like them.
I hate him.
And
I hate my name on the board

The psychologist says
"He's a kinesthetic child.
Pencils just tap when he's
  around."

My teacher says
"ADAM!"

and I'm Adam X again
and I bloody hate it.

© *Brian Vince, 1999 – used with the author's permission*

▪ Reward systems seem to work best when three conditions are met: the classroom is generally stress-free; the tasks are essentially non-creative or routine and require only low-level skills; and the behaviour, not the person, is rewarded. Outside of these conditions they are self-defeating in the long term. Besides, the rewards that most children want are not material ones but the relational ones of friendliness, warmth, acceptance, recognition, encouragement and the good opinion of others. (The reward most children cite as the most desirable is positive feedback from their parents.) In addition, to be really effective, such relational rewarding should be spontaneous and unpredictable and not be linked to task accomplishment. Not a common strategy employed in classrooms! Punishments are often the removal of these relational rewards. The positive goal of any reward/sanction programme is ultimately that the children learn that behaviours are a matter of choice and that choices have benefits and losses, desirable and undesirable consequences. And that is the key lesson to be learned.

Discipline versus counselling

The approaches in the spectrum of theories at the beginning of this section can also be differentiated as to whether their method of improving behaviour leans more towards discipline than counselling. A discipline system can be thought of as an organisational intervention high on teacher responsibility, which focuses on the behaviour; while counselling approaches focus on the *intention* behind the behaviour. A disciplinary intervention can be quick and immediate. However, discipline systems can degenerate into an equivalence to punishment systems rather than grow into a way of leadership – leadership that is in terms of steering students to a greater level of self-responsibility. A counselling intervention focuses more on pupil self-responsibility and presupposes sufficient time is available to intervene successfully. Time is needed to develop self-awareness and the self-management skills to achieve the mature, responsible learner.

The pressure of time in schools accounts for the growing popularity of "brief" approaches to counselling as well as that of peer counselling. There is some evidence that older children make good counsellors with a higher level of active listening ability than might be expected. Some schools in Birmingham, UK, have introduced peer mediators to help resolve playground disputes. Their training has contributed to their development of communication skills, emotional intelligence and their self-management skills. Teachers report raised levels of self-esteem and a higher order of social competence.

*Assertive discipline approaches (see Canter and Canter) are based on clear behavioural rules and an accompanying hierarchy of sanctions with positive feedback for compliance to the rules. This has been shown to produce more "on-task" behaviour, a lower incidence of disruptive conduct and an increase in teacher praise. It rests on a set of assumptions and beliefs that include:

- that nowadays pupils do not come to school with a respect for authority, and therefore …
- the classroom needs to be managed by the teacher, so that …
- the teacher's key role is to manage the environment by …
- teaching compliance to the teacher's rules.

In some schools this approach has degenerated into a preference for the short-term benefits of removing a child over the longer-term benefits to be gained from the development of a good working relationship and the more complex task of conflict resolution. It becomes a path of least resistance, avoiding the problem rather than solving it to promote growth. However, rewards and sanctions can change behaviour superficially when the child decides that the reward is worth getting or the punishment worth avoiding. This promotes the mental set of "what's in it for me?", which can then produce compliant behaviour. Our target is *committed* learning not *compliant* learning! More durable behaviour changes are possible if the person internalises the reasons for the change, i.e., gets them to change how they *think* about their behaviour. In the Dilts model this means thinking at a level higher than the behaviour level (see the Einstein example in Chapter One, page 11).

Research by Barbara Maines showed the power of language in a study she made of pupils whose behaviour was considered difficult. She trained a group of eleven teachers to adjust the way they gave instructions to their pupils. They were asked always to:

- Use the child's name and establish good eye contact before giving the child the instruction;
- Avoid the usual classroom jargon and typical teacher-coded talk;
- Check for understanding before going on to …;
- Ask the child to restate the instructions in her own words.

Just by adherence to these simple rules, the measured incidence of disruptive or off-task behaviour was halved. Basically, the three key elements of good communication were present – of greater clarity of language, set within a good relational context, with feedback on the receiver's understanding (see NLP principle number 6 in Chapter One, page 6) – to produce appropriate behaviour. The over-all message for me from this study is that this improved level of communication reduced the level of anxiety that the child faced in confronting new learning and therefore contributed to more successful behaviour management.

The psychology of behaviour and learning – a toolkit of ideas and practices

Behaviours are just the tip of the hidden iceberg of a person's inner emotions. They are however, your best guide to the inner state of the other person. Children are born to be social animals. Therein lies survival for our species. If children consistently behave antisocially, it is generally because their innermost needs are not being met. Modern scientists consider there are four primary emotions – *fear, anger, sorrow* and *parental love* – that determine our behaviours or reactions to the events of our world. For children in a classroom we could relabel these as *fear, anger, sadness* and *happiness* or just plain feeling "bad, mad, sad and glad".

The emotional state of happiness may be thought of as the absence of the first three, but it is more than that. Certainly, the child needs to be free of the first three socially negative emotions to reach this state, but happiness is connected more positively to needs fulfil-ment. These primary emotions are linked to the bodily effects that are produced by the part of the brain known as the *amygdala*. In a now superseded (but still useful) model of the brain, scientists referred to the lower or stem part of the brain as the reptilian brain because they thought it was its most primitive part. The midbrain was considered the seat of our emotions and the upper part, the cortex, the centre of our thinking. Although this is now recognised as a simplistic model, three of our main life-driving forces can still be thought of as the brain's:

- Desire for safety or wish to avoid harm (the main job of the lower brain);
- Its hunt for pleasure (the aim of the mid-brain), and;
- Its quest for, and curiosity about, the new (the concern of the upper brain, the cortex).

The amygdala can be thought of as the instinctive part of the brain – the inbuilt survival-control mechanism that exists in all animals. Its primary task is to respond to events that may pose a threat to your survival. It appraises the incoming data and prepares the body for action by governing the hormone flows that prompt and allow you to flee from danger, to oppose it or to submit to it. In modern society, our daily experiences do not often involve meetings with predators. However, the same physiological effects that result in flight from, fight with or submission to a predator are still visible as we do things such as drive a car, compete with colleagues at interview or undergo a school inspection! Psychologists recognise that these physiological effects are still produced daily and associate them with our underlying anxieties about survival in our social interactions in the modern world. They are classified in Table 3.2.

Table 3.2: The three basic social anxieties

Behaviour	Emotion	Associated anxiety
Fight	Anger	Performance & control anxiety (related to issues around myself and the answers to the question of "What am I?")
Submission	Sorrow	Acceptance & inclusion anxiety (addressing the question of "Who am I?" in relation to others)
Flight	Fear	Orientation & personal goal anxiety (fear of being lost and confused and the answers to the questions "Where am I? What sort of world is this?")

Each anxiety distorts "normal" behaviour patterns into corresponding "driven" behaviours, not least because with each primary reaction comes a change in body chemistry. As we prepare to fight, so the volume of the chemical noradrenaline in the body, rises, with blood vessels being constricted, while submission is accompanied by a large rise in cortisol levels. Preparation for flight sees rises in both these two but is accompanied by an even bigger rise in adrenaline. Sustained high levels of each of these chemicals can result in physical damage over time.

In the classroom, the anxieties also produce "stuck" behaviour patterns because, after we have developed them and had success in their use in one instance, we often just repeat them in new circumstances. This can continue long after they have ceased to be useful. Also, because many of our distorted behaviour patterns stem from experiences earlier in life (their antecedents), the emotions associated with the earlier experience can be triggered by some action of another person. How often have you recalled a traumatic event by saying, "I panicked and my mind went a complete blank"? This is because, as anxiety levels rise, so the blood drains from the cortex, the thinking part of the brain, and concentrates in the brain's emotional centre, the limbic system. At this point the person under stress often falls back on old behaviour patterns, which may not be the best solution to the current crisis. You cannot think "logically" in a highly emotionally charged state.

One of the effects of both the emotional state and the reliance on old behaviour patterns is that the person begins to communicate less effectively. The more emotions take over, the less coherent the communication. This can then deepen the misunderstanding. To move on you will need to let go of the anxiety. So it is with the child – and the teacher's role is to intervene in a way that "unsticks" the child (Figure 3.1). For a teacher working with a child, language is the key to reversing the process and unlocking that stuck state. And some words and phrases are more potent than others in taking a child to a more resourceful state of mind. A relaxed, anxiety-free and accepting mind, was for Georgi Lozanov, the ideal learning state.

Just as the original emotional drivers have as their positive intention, our physical survival, so these social anxieties also have a positive intention – they exist to protect our self-esteem. Self-esteem

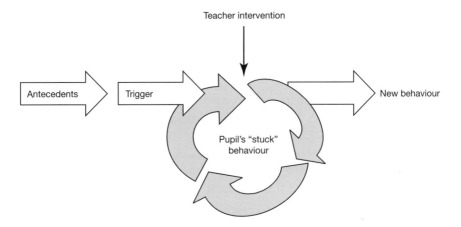

Figure 3.1: A model of teacher–pupil interaction

and anxiety are often two sides of the same coin. In 1989, Lord Elton reported that "our evidence suggests that many children who behave badly are those whose self-esteem is threatened by failure". Children's behaviour is naturalistically directed towards situations and experiences that enhance or maintain the sense of self-worth or allow them to achieve. To raise a child's self-esteem you first have to know how she values herself and what "success" is in her mental map of the world. And this is often the clue to the primary latent anxiety, just as the anxiety is often the pointer to the way to raise self-esteem.

Anxiety is a fear of the future and, when it reaches a threshold level, it will trigger a sequence of almost automatic responses. That is, a state of being which contains elements of a hypnotic trance. The child hallucinates positively, by projecting forward into the future to envisage a disaster scenario; or negatively, by failing to see resources or alternative ways forward. Both can result in the child giving itself posthypnotic commands or suggestions to start limiting self-talk: "I won't be able to do it", "People will laugh at me" etc. The sorts of questions that arise in children's minds at these times that affect their self-esteem and are linked to these anxieties when they surface in the classroom are:

- **Performance and control anxiety:** Will I be able to do what I have to do? Will I be up to it? Will I be able to control the situation to meet my needs?

- **Orientation anxiety:** Will I understand what's going on? Will I be able to make sense of it? Will my contribution be wanted?
- **Acceptance and inclusion anxiety:** Will I be liked? Will I like the others? Will I be allowed to stay in this class?

These questions point towards virtual goals – goals that the child desires but may be consciously unaware of, or unable to articulate. For performance anxiety the need is for control and the goals are recognition, kudos and perceived status. For orientation anxiety there is a need for achievement and the goal success. For acceptance/inclusion anxiety the needs are social and the goals such things as compliments and praise from teachers and peers. These are goals that you as a teacher can convert into basic entitlements for every child you teach and use as principles that underpin your teaching. Look at Anna, Billy, Chris and David in Exercise 3.1. What were the primary anxieties for each case? What are their important questions? What is their unexpressed need?

Learning, almost by definition, is going to be an anxiety-producing activity, since it presupposes that you are proceeding into unknown territory, into areas of your ignorance or those in which you are currently unable to do what is needed. You are leaving your comfort zone and moving through your zone of proximal development towards new territory. A learning path is likely to entail confusion, uncertainty, frustration and sometimes disappointment. All of these may threaten your self-esteem. It is not surprising, therefore, that learning can be something to be avoided; that so many people seek simple answers to complex questions; that many of us give up certain learning paths.

Mihaly Csikszentmihalyi (1996) describes the territory between anxiety and boredom as "flow" – a time when everything just progresses harmoniously. In learning, it is the place of balance between the threat of the unknown and the boredom of the known bordered by Piaget's states of rejection and assimilation. It is his area of possible assimilation. There may be considerable unsteadiness within that area, with the path sometimes moving back and forth between the two boundaries. The teacher's role is to help students maintain that state of flow and extend their learning and achieve their full potential (see Figure 3.2).

Exercise 3.1: Anxiety

Consider the following scenes:

- Anna is doing a graphics projection, following the teacher's instructions on how to do it, when she takes a wrong step and comes to a dead end. "How does she expect me to do this when she never explains things properly?" she asks herself, and then feels angry. She bangs her pencil down on the table and stops doing the task.

- Billy is reading in class when he realises that other children on the table are looking at him and laughing. He thinks of them as friends, and begins to feel miserable that they should be making fun of him and starts to stumble over the words. His reading dries up.

- Chris is drawing a still life as part of an observation-skills exercise, when she looks across at Janice sitting next to her. Janice's drawing is much more realistic than hers and she feels ashamed of her own effort. She begins to scribble aimlessly and shade over the drawing.

- David is drilling out a piece of wood when the drill bit snaps. He's surprised and frightened about what to do next. He hurriedly tugs the broken bit out of the wood and hides it in his pocket. He then looks around to see if he can put the drill back before the teacher notices.

Choose one of these stories and re-read it, putting yourself in Anna's, Billy's, Chris's or David's shoes. As you come to the end, ask yourself:

- How am I feeling and what am I thinking?

- Would I do what my character would have done?

- Would I have been able to carry on with my learning/task?

- What would I have done in each case to kick-start my learning?

These little stories illustrate that our inner feelings such as fear, anger and grief, drive our behaviours.

Those children whose behaviour springs from a performance anxiety need to be told that they are doing or have done a good job. Those who are concerned about caring need reassurance that they are cared for, or that they have done a good job in looking after or helping others. Those with an orientation anxiety need to be told that their actions were crucial in helping others understand and

Table 3.3:   Positive intentions and entitlements

Anxiety	Positive intention	Perceived entitlement
Performance & control anxiety	Personal freedom & task accomplishment	To be free to make decisions for oneself
Acceptance & inclusion anxiety	Chance to care and be cared for	To belong and to be respected and loved for oneself as an individual
Orientation & personal-goal anxiety	Desire to contribute	To make a contribution to play one's part and be seen to be significant

accomplish the task. You can think about your own classroom and ask yourself:

- How and when are the students acknowledged as important in themselves by being free to take decisions about their learning?
- How and where are the children cared for in this room?
- How and in what ways do pupils contribute to their own learning and to that of their peers?

In painting, children learn to generate the whole spectrum of colours from the three primary pigments, red, blue and yellow. We seem to be able to generate our secondary emotions in the same way – so, for instance, shame could be thought of as sorrow with a little fear; jealousy as fear with a little anger. Such secondary emotions are not so much instinctive as learned. They are a result of the meanings we have attached to our experiences in life. They are therefore within our control provided we learn to make choices about our emotional state. The current focus on emotional education is an acknowledgment of the importance of the part we play in managing our personal emotional state.

For simplicity's sake in explaining these ideas, I have treated people as if they could be grouped according to their dominant anxieties into just these three groups. In life, we know that people are not so easily categorised, but this simplicity helps us begin to apply the model in real situations. Increased sophistication comes with usage and experience. We can make the model a little more flexible by

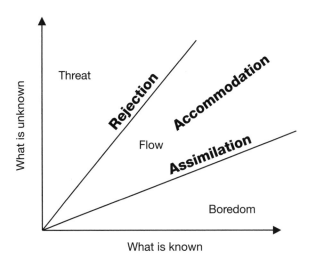

Figure 3.2: Flow

introducing three other subdivisions of the anxieties. We can consider those people who have two anxieties of relatively equal
strength – say fear plus sorrow, anger plus sorrow or anger plus
fear. That is, they can have the blended needs of:

- *Performance and caring* – these people want to get the task done to
  their satisfaction, but also want to help others get there too.
- *Performance and orientation* – this time, these people need to get
  the task done but will do so by concentrating on a thought-
  through process or strategy designed to accomplish it.
- *Orientation and caring* – these people will attempt to help
  others, particularly to help those people to help themselves; at
  the same time, however, they will not risk their own autonomy
  in doing so.

In changing behaviour, Robert Dilts's model (Figure 1.3) points up
what teachers do instinctively already – never to mistake behaviour
for identity. All good teachers know to distinguish very carefully
between behaviours that are inappropriate in the environment of
the classroom, and the child as someone who is innately OK as a
worthwhile human being in their own right. However, the model
adds more layers to common practice. It indicates that it is also vital
to separate an unwanted behaviour from the driving intention or

belief behind it. The behaviour might be bad in the circumstances, but the intention is likely to be positive in some respect.

William Glasser in his "choice theory" of behaviour says that "everything we do is initiated by a satisfying picture of that activity that we store in our heads as a pleasant memory". With our knowledge of NLP we can extend that definition to recognise the fact that for some children the memory may be stored as a feeling or as sounds, rather than as a picture. By "satisfying" he means achieving a goal, because, whatever the modality, the person will always have a goal in mind. It may be in or beneath the child's conscious awareness (in the unconscious mind). Another dimension that NLP brings to choice theory is the recognition that the particular behaviour might stem from a self-limiting belief. The child mistakenly believes that this specific behaviour is the only or best way available to him at the time! Being aware of the positive intention and the desired goal is the first step in helping a child perceive that there are likely to be alternative ways of satisfying the intention and achieving the goal. So a key teacher skill is the ability to open up the child's mental map to help them recognise and/or devise new avenues to reach the goal.

Dilts has used his model to tease out the role a teacher best plays at the different levels to improve the child's development. Although you can, and will, switch between these different roles while teaching *any* age group, these different modes of teaching are strongly related to age development. They start with more emphasis on being the caretaker and coach in the early years of schooling, through teacher and mentor in the middle years and to sponsor and awakener at the young adult stage.

Underpinning all three key behaviours of fight, flight and submission as they are exhibited in the classroom is a mistaken belief – the belief that the behaviour will get you the corresponding positive goals of self-determination, achievement and acceptance, respectively. John Heron (1989) argues that these goals often stem from early experiences in the child's life that have resulted in hidden emotions. Fight – from repressed anger at the limits imposed on one's own self-expression; flight – from repressed fear of the threats to one's own identity; and submission – from the repressed sadness at receiving insufficient love and regard. If these older sources of

Table 3.4: The spectrum of teaching roles

Level	Role	Behaviour
Community	Awakener	The *teacher as awakener* is someone who provides the learning experiences that deepens the learner's understanding of what it is to be human, to be a social being, while demonstrating his own humanity
Identity	Sponsor	The *teacher as sponsor* is the person who gives the learner space to be himself, who supports him in understanding that it is OK to be who he is, with his own unique values, beliefs and abilities
Beliefs/values	Mentor	The role of mentor includes advising and counselling the student as he develops his beliefs and values and who guides him by example
Capability	Teacher	The core task of enlarging the knowledge of the children, developing their skills and extending their capabilities
Behaviour	Coach	The teacher as improver of performance; of providing the feedback to refine skills and competences
Environment	Caretaker	The teacher as provider of a good learning environment; of securing a safe, anxiety-free climate for learning

distress are present, then they will drive the presenting behaviour more powerfully. Even if they are not, all teachers recognise a more immediate form of emotional distress – embarrassment. This is a conditioned fear of other people's opinions of you, the fear that, if they found out what the real you is like, they would not like you. Embarrassment usually cloaks one or more of the three basic anxieties. Some of the behavioural clues that point to the anxiety or the mental interferences are:

Performance and control
- Competes with others to do better than they do, needs to win and may cheat to do so
- Manipulates others and may brag, blame or tease
- Looks for high-profile "public" goals
- Takes risks
- Hates failing and tends to perfectionism

The internal conflict between these last two can lead to lower levels of aspiration and commitment to tasks, if it means being able to remain in control or to stand out from the crowd. Children with extremes of misbehaviour stemming from this anxiety are often typified as bullies or rebels.

Acceptance and inclusion

- Desires to "fit in" and may give away toys, sweets or money to "buy" into a group
- Avoids of confrontation and is often apologetic
- Has expectations/aspirations linked to peer set standards and norms
- Complies with and supports group goals to the point of acting silly
- Constantly apologises

The individual potential and achievement are lowered if the group standards are low so as not to stand out from the crowd. Children in this category are perceived as "hangers-on" or "easily led", and at the extremes become "loners", being withdrawn or isolated.

Orientation and personal goal

- Strives to do better and can be heavily self-critical
- Seeks a lot of feedback
- Takes only moderate risks
- Demonstrates moderate to low levels of initiative taking

For some pupils this anxiety can lead to a fixing of low internally imposed standards to minimise the perception of failure. They often indulge in "distraction" or task-avoidance behaviours – jocularity, gossip, chattering about irrelevancies, doing trivial activities. You can look back at the stories of Anna, Bill, Chris and David in Exercise 3.1 and notice the driving anxiety behind each scenario.

If you have ever acted as a mentor to a student or newly qualified teacher you will have experienced the situation in which the student teacher has, through their own inexperience, escalated an incident into deep conflict. The different anxieties give rise to easily spotted patterns of behaviour that can spiral out of control if not handled properly and promptly. Since the different anxieties have the different perceived expected entitlements outlined above, if these are not met or they are devalued in some way, then we have all the conditions for conflict as a "violation of expectations". So being denied the chance to make decisions for oneself or being prevented from getting on with the job because of the teacher's perceived interference or inability to provide the necessary tools and resources is going to be a trigger for those with a performance anxiety.

Being prevented from supporting others in the group, being given insufficient one-to-one time, being unappreciated will worry those students with inclusion anxiety uppermost. Being given only vague instructions, being uncertain of their role, being rushed and prevented from doing a good job or being overdirected will rattle those with fears about their personal understanding of the goals set them. They are all breeding grounds for conflict. If the difference in expectations is not resolved, each anxiety gives rise to a predictable pattern of behaviours in handling conflict, related to the perceived threat to the individual's self-esteem.

When faced with tension between their own needs and the needs of someone else, those people who aren't skilful enough to work to a win/win situation will usually first seek a way out of their dilemma through compromise. They will attempt to split the difference – a win some/lose some situation. If this doesn't succeed, then the next step is usually in one of three directions dependent on the dominant anxiety. People whose dominant anxiety is that of acceptance will, if the stakes are high enough, give in to the demands of the other person – they submit, they "freeze". Ostensibly, this is a "lose" for them, a "win" for the other. However this outcome preserves their own sense of being "liked" by the winner. Someone with an orientation anxiety will go in to flight, will go to any lengths to avoid the face-to-face. That way, there is no competition, so there are no winners. However, in human relational terms, both have lost an opportunity to take their relationship to a higher level. For those with a performance anxiety, their self-esteem is based on not losing, so, if pushed will compete: "If you force me into a choice between me and you, then *I* have to come out on top."

You can get linguistic clues and behavioural clues to the driving anxiety.

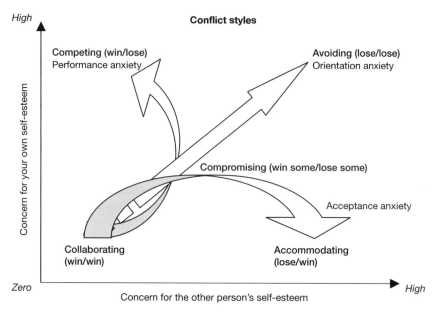

Figure 3.3: Patterns of conflict behaviour

Which of the five behaviours is your strength in confrontation? Such strengths, when overdone, become weaknesses. Exercise 3.3 will give you a very approximate profile of your preferred approaches. (A more sophisticated instrument, the Thomas–Kilman Conflict Mode Instrument, is available in most general books on self-development for managers.)

The neurological-level model (see Figure 1.3 on page 12) is also a particularly powerful aid in analysing the full context of the child's misbehaviour as the first step in designing an intervention to improve it. It helps us frame a set of questions that take us from the antecedents and triggers of Figure 3.1 (page 79), through the anxieties and the mistaken beliefs, to the positive intentions. The answers to the questions of Table 3.7 help determine the most likely level for successful intervention.

Being aware of the starting points and the end points of the child that are outside the classroom context, their driving anxieties and their goals allows us to construct a model for bringing about new, more acceptable behaviours.

Table 3.5: Anxiety-driven strategies for handling conflict

Anxiety	Perceived threat level		
	Low	**Medium**	**High**
Acceptance & inclusion anxiety	Will accommodate other person's needs within their own (their form of compromise or win some/lose some)	Will give way to	Will give up
Self-esteem rating	*(You are OK, I am not OK – so I had better let you have your way)*		
			SUBMISSION
Performance & control anxiety	Will raise their game and increase efforts to complete the task (their form of compromise or win some/lose some)	Will begin to compete with others to best them and win (win/lose)	Will fight aggressively
Self-esteem rating	*(I am OK, you are not OK – so I want my own way)*		
			RETALIATION
Orientation & personal-goal anxiety	Will go cautiously to minimise risk to task or to themselves (their form of compromise or win some/lose some	Will try to get out of doing the task (lose/lose)	Will retreat from the situation
Self-esteem rating	*(I am not OK, you are not OK – I wish it weren't a question of either me or you)*		
			ESCAPE

Table 3.6: Conflict and language

Type	Emotional response	Language
Competer	Anger/attack (*Fight*)	It's your fault ..., If you had/hadn't ..., You were supposed to ...
Avoider	Fear/defensive (*Flight*)	No, I didn't ..., It's not my fault ..., I couldn't help it ... OR just silence
Accommodator	Sadness/apologetic (*Freeze*)	I'm sorry ... (even when it's not their fault); Please forgive me ..., You're still my friend?, I won't do it again ...
Collaborator	Confidence (*Flow*)	How can we both ...?

At the same time we should also be aware of our own anxieties and the degree to which they might distort our own behaviour and limit our capacity to deal adequately with the situation. For a teacher, the basic anxieties can have the behaviour distortions of Table 3.8.

Bill Rogers, in his behaviour-recovery programme, makes the point that at the teacher-intervention stage we sometimes forget that new behaviours often have to be taught. Just as reading and writing

Table 3.7: Questions at the different neurological levels

Community	How do the other pupils in the class view the behaviour? How do other teachers in the school view the behaviour?
Identity	How does the pupil see herself? What does the pupil feel or think about herself in behaving like this?
Beliefs/values	What does behaving like this *mean* for her? What value does it have for her? What outcome does she believe this behaviour will gain for her?
Capabilities	What skills might she need to learn, develop or improve to get the desired behaviour?
Behaviour	What specifically does she do or say? (Describe it in behavioural or sensory terms – without judgments or nominalisations.)
Environment	What are the situational factors surrounding this behaviour? When does it happen (and what happens just before it appears)?

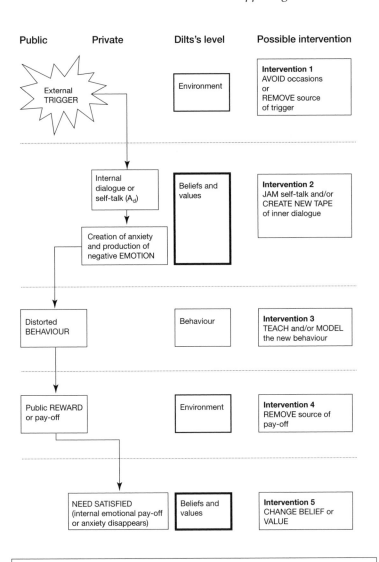

Figure 3.4: Misbehaviour strategy and teacher interventions

Table 3.8: The four Fs of behaviour and teacher-distorted responses to conflict
For a teacher, the basic anxieties can have the following distortions:

Emotion	Associated anxiety	Distorted behaviour in the classroom	The four Fs of behaviour
Anger	Performance and control anxiety	Aggressively handling the issue or "clobbering" the other person *getting MAD in the confrontation*	Fight
Sorrow	Acceptance/and inclusion anxiety	Avoiding any confrontation *feeling SAD at the situation*	Freeze
Fear	Orientation and personal goal anxiety	"Pussyfooting" around the real issue *feeling BAD about having to confront*	Flight

Only when these three are absent do you get:

Happiness	Anxiety-free behaviour	Undistorted behaviour shown by willingness to confront the situation and handle it assertively *Just GLAD to see confrontation as a chance to improve the relationship*	Flow or simply *Fun!*

have to be taught through small incremental steps, so change and improvement in behaviour has also to be worked at. This parallels Don Blackerby's reminder (1996) that *how* to learn or do something also has to be taught. In that teaching, I believe it is possible to bring about changes in behaviour, "conversationally". The belief that words *do* work is the key intervention strategy advocated throughout this book. The basic rules of this behavioural training approach are:

1. Use language that is in the modalities preferred by the child for perceiving and communicating about the world; this means using the predicate words of the preferred modality.
2. Use the child's motivational patterns (meta-programs) to strengthen the commitment to change.

3. Use metaphors to improve and extend understanding.
4. Reinforce verbal communication with nonverbal signals.

Experiments in training children in managing their own behaviour have been very successful and have demonstrated long-term improvement (Berliner and Casanova, 1993). The most creative and productive way of teaching new behaviour is based on the sequence:

- Modelling – demonstrating the desired behaviour oneself;
- Rehearsal – giving the child the opportunity to practise the behaviour;
- Cueing – signalling when it is appropriate to use the new behaviour;
- Reinforcement– catching/praising the child when they exhibit the behaviour and not criticising them in its absence.

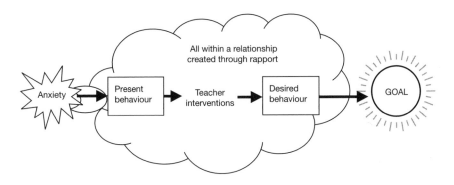

Figure 3.5: A linear model of behaviour change

An approach that uses this process to improve behaviour in the classroom is *circle* time. This had been introduced into the teacher's repertoire over the 1990s. With its focus on communication and cooperation within a group, self-expression and the working through of individual and group issues, it supports the social and moral development of children as a peer learning group. The teacher can model the desired behaviours, and the process allows for repeated opportunities for children to practise with positive reinforcement. This has many benefits. One of the most obvious is the development of listening skills through practice.

Many behavioural problems arise out of poor listening between peers and between child and teacher.

A second is the development of the skills that underpin emotional intelligence. Circle time emphasises the growth in knowledge and management of the child's own emotions and the recognition and acceptance of the emotions of the others in the group. It brings a structured, nondefensive approach to handling relationships. Most important of all, is that a well-conducted circle time allows children the space to address the fundamental needs of inclusion, acceptance and freedom. They all have the freedom within the circle-time rules to speak and be listened to; to express opinions, which can be heard nonjudgmentally; and to be respected – all key elements of self-esteem and the foundation skills of emotional intelligence. They get positive peer feedback and the encouragement to recognise their capacity to change. From an NLP perspective, it offers an opportunity to unpick labels, particularly negative ones, and distinguish once again between behaviours and identity. For the teacher, it is an ideal opportunity to figure out where the child is coming from, to experiment with recognising and using the language patterns learned from this book.

Brain research

Brain development is a process of increasingly making and remaking connections between neurons to set up three-dimensional spider webs of neural pathways in the brain. Which paths are strengthened and which parts atrophy depends on what the child experiences in their environment. The build-up of new pathways outpaces the disappearance of old ones for the first eight months after birth, until there are about twenty times more than there were when the baby was born. The pre-frontal cortex, where our rational thinking occurs, forms more and more connections, using twice as much energy as an adult brain to do so, for the next ten years.

In the second year of the baby's life, the withering of paths outstrips the new growth until, by the end of the second year, the overall number has halved and the baby has about the same number of synapses as an adult. The child's environment and its experiences over this year shape which connections are reinforced and which disappear or diminish. A well-functioning cortex (the upper part of the brain) is necessary for learning and depends on the healthy growth of the midbrain and the brain stem – the parts that govern the emotional wellbeing of the child. The cortex remains more plastic and adaptable to new experience throughout life. However, the brain stem, which *organises* the brain, becomes less plastic and so the experiences of the child's first two years strongly determine the future functioning of the child.

The brain's normal healthy answer to alarming situations is one or other of the well-known fight, freeze or flight responses. Young children exposed to traumatic situations often adopt an exaggerated form of one of these responses. Later, in classrooms, this can be seen in children who are inappropriately aggressive in their relationships with others, or are passive and noninteractive in their behaviour. Scientists think this is because such trauma and other negative experiences in a child's early life can affect the development and structure of the brain. Specifically it seems to prevent the build-up of neural links. Experimenters and educators have shown that these changes can be reversed if the child becomes the subject of an intensive programme of care and activities.

Earlier research on patients who had damaged one or other of the two cerebral hemispheres led to the idea of hemisphere dominance and the concepts of right- and left-brain thinking. Experiments showed that there seemed to be two quite distinct ways in which the brain processed information. One was a step-by-step, sequential way of processing ascribed to the left side of the brain, and the other a holistic, simultaneous way of processing, ascribed to the right. The respective hemispheres were thought of as the logical, analytical brain and the creative, intuitive, pattern-seeking brain. We now know that this is too simplistic an interpretation of the brain's actual functioning, since all of the brain is involved to differing extents in the mind's processing of sensory data.

Scientists currently make models of the brain's functioning based on developments in other scientific research. For example, some scientists liken the brain to a hologram. A holographic plate does not contain a recognisable image on its surface, but an indecipherable mist of swirling shaded patterning. And yet, under the correct lighting, it re-forms to construct a 3-D image. This image is both everywhere and yet nowhere on the plate. This means that unlike a photograph, if you break the plate in two, it won't give two different halves of the one image. Both pieces will give you back the whole image. Applying this model to a memory, for instance, neuroscientists argue that it is not filed in some corner of the brain to be retrieved when needed, but is reconstructed anew from unrecognisably coded data from all over the brain each time it is needed, just like a hologram. Other scientists see the laws of complexity theory at work in the brain and consider that memories and ideas could be the result of "ordered" synchronous firing of neural pathways emerging out of the otherwise apparently continuous, chaotic electrical activity of the brain.

Whatever the model, the idea of these two polarised approaches to intellectual thought can be useful when we first think about learning and behaviour. We can see it reflected in McCarthy's 4-MAT description of learning styles (see Figure 1.5). More importantly, we can see it in the classroom. Younger children operate for much of the time in what was thought of as "right-brain" mode – they doodle, paint and daydream, and talk to imaginary friends. Schooling at this stage begins to encourage, and eventually impose, "left-brain" thinking – just think of the British government's institution of the literacy hour and the numeracy strategy. The practical application of this model in the classroom would suggest that, to prompt either of the two processes separately or to stimulate both of them simultaneously, you could, for the "right" brain:

- Start with story/jokes related to the material;
- Provide opportunities for learning by discovery;
- Allow opportunities for small group work;
- Use tactile resources, role play, diagrams and pictures;
- Provide specific objectives.

For the "left" brain:

- Give clear instructions;
- Provide written reinforcement of messages on the board/ flipchart;
- Encourage the independent use of resources;
- Step through the details;
- Use concept maps.

For the whole brain:

- Combine words and pictures with colours;
- Combine words and numbers with music;
- Encourage visualisation/imagination;
- Use background music when presenting or reviewing information.

It is this more holistic approach to learning, which utilises both polarities, that is the basis of accelerated-learning strategies.

Another aspect of research into the brain's functioning is that of the differences in its electrical flow patterns during different activities. Four main patterns have been observed and classified as:

1. **Beta** (waves of 14–25 Hertz (Hz) or cycles/second): Normal, everyday, wakefulness consisting of rational thoughts, distractions and scattered thoughts, all passing through our internal filters and subject to our meta-programs. These come to the fore when anxiety levels rise.

2. **Alpha** (8–14 Hz): A focused state of alertness where the patterns of both left and right hemispheres are in step. Time and space limitations often seem to disappear – it is the state in which we often lose our sense of time.

3. **Theta** (4–8 Hz): The sleep state, going from light to deep sleep, in which we dream and into which our subconscious mind often intrudes. Brilliant insights often leap out of this brain state. These are the brain rhythms of the state that mystics or healers work to create consciously in their healing rituals.

4. **Delta** (less than 4 Hz): Very deep sleep, moving towards coma.

The higher frequencies associated with conscious thoughts and left-hemisphere processing can result in stress. You can think too much! It is also known that the best state for learning can be described as an alert yet relaxed frame of mind, which is associated with the alpha frequencies. It is at these frequencies that the mind seems to be at its most creative, making most use of combining the sequential reasoning of the left hemisphere with the new insights emerging from the right hemisphere. Both sides of the brain are "in tune".

In the last few years a technique called neuro-feedback has been developed, in which subjects are taught to control their own brain rhythms. In 2000, 22 musicians from the Royal College of Music in London were taught how to create a relaxed brain state, using a computer game that responded to the electrical activity in their heads to help them stimulate alpha rhythms. After receiving the training they were asked to rate their own performances and found that the quality of their music making, their emotional commitment to it and their interpretive imagination had all improved.

The same methods are now being used with children classified as having attention-deficit hyperactivity disorder (ADHD). You may not have the technology in your classroom to replicate this training, but you can help stimulate alpha-wave production by careful use of language – by what you say and how you say it.

Emotional intelligence – for you and them

Educating for emotional intelligence has two main skill objectives: the improvement of the individual's management of their own emotional state (a personal competence) and the management of the relationships with others (a social competence). The emotionally skilled teacher is competent in both these areas, able to manage their emotions to create conditions for learning. As a teacher, you understand that the primary determinant of the classroom climate is the emotional relationship between child and teacher and not the cognitive factors. Therefore, becoming more aware of your own feelings, your own internal emotional state, and then managing/altering it allows you to maintain your own behavioural flexibility and resourcefulness in the face of a demanding student.

What is going on inside you when you interact with a pupil who is misbehaving? How might this affect your ability to deal with the situation effectively? We sometimes stick too rigidly to linear thinking – to think only in terms of cause–effect, of situational trigger and response. It could be better to move to "circular" thinking – to see if this behaviour is part of a longer-term cycle of events. Do *you* have repeating cycles of responding to situations? If so, you may need to break them in order to be successful in managing behaviour. It often helps to be very clear about your own intentions when intervening. Work through the tracking exercise (Exercise 3.2) to become aware of your responses.

Rupert Dreikurs (1984) suggests that as you become aware of your feelings you could link them to possible reasons for why the pupil is behaving as they do. He proposed that, if you feel merely irritated by the behaviour, the child is an attention seeker; if you feel challenged, the child is a power seeker; if you feel hurt, the child is a revenge seeker; if you feel exasperated, the child is playing "helpless". He also suggested useful matching teacher interventions to handle the behaviour. You can draw some rough parallels with this analysis and the primary anxieties:

- The power seeker equates to the *performance-and-control* anxiety – their self-esteem depends on their level of self-determination in their work.

- The revenge seeker equates to the *orientation* anxiety – they need to feel significant, even if that is only through hurting the teacher; they fear, so they will seek to frighten.

- The attention seeker equates to the *acceptance-and-inclusion* anxiety – their self-esteem depends on their level of perceived acceptance into the group.

- The "inadequate" also links to the *acceptance-and-inclusion* anxiety – they feel they can belong only if they show their need for the group's support.

Although this classification is in line with what is offered in this book, there are some fundamental differences between the two approaches. It runs counter to a number of NLP principles outlined in Part I. For instance, it makes the linguistic equivalence between the person and his behaviour – "power seeker", "revenge seeker" and so on, when my NLP principle number 2 in Chapter One says "people are not their behaviour". It also ascribes negative motivations behind the behaviour – revenge, hurt – when NLP principle number 3 asks you to behave as though you believed that every behaviour has a positive intention behind it at some level. In Part III, I describe the use of nominalisations (nouns derived from verbs – such as the Dreikurs descriptors) and presuppositions (unspoken assumptions that lie behind words) and their potentially corrosive

Exercise 3.2: Personal emotional competence – a tracking exercise

Think back to a situation when you last faced a student, a situation you didn't handle well, one in which your own intervention or behaviour didn't help the situation, where you left the encounter, having lost track for a minute or two of the lesson and what you were meant to be doing next with the rest of the class. If you have been in a situation like that, imagine it had been videoed, and rerun the tape of the situation in your mind. Then:

1. First, go inside and just *notice* what is going on inside your body:

   • Has your breathing changed? Is it faster, slower, deeper, shallower?

   • Are any of your muscles tensed or feeling stiff?

   • Is your mouth open or closed?

   • Is your jaw clenched or relaxed?

2. Now *become aware* of your emotional state:

   • How are you feeling?

   • What are you feeling – angry, tense, frustrated, sad, disappointed, irritated, ashamed, guilty …?

   • Where in your body is the emotion located?

3. Check your internal dialogue:

   • What self-talk tapes are running?

   • What are your thinking and saying to yourself?

4. Now come back outside *and bring your attention to the present:*

   • Where are you?

   • Notice your surroundings: what's happening around you?

5. *Change* what you were doing – think of the future, the direction in which you want to go, the outcome you want, rather than what happened in the past incident:

   • What outcome do you want? Get a picture in your mind's eye of how you envisage it. What are the other people around you saying? What is the positive feeling you want at that time?

6. *Keep tracking* what is going on inside for you, how your feelings are shifting, and do what you need to do in order to get into or to remain in a calm, relaxed and yet alert state.

This is one way of finding out your own "hot-buttons" – the ones that result in knee-jerk reactions or distorted behaviour. These are those personal buttons that children instinctively know how to press in all their teachers.

When you know them, you are prepared for your next encounter with that student and can focus on what you need to do, how you need to behave to move your relationship onto a better footing to improve the behaviour.

effect on everyday normal communication. In that section, you can explore the beneficial use of these linguistic tools.

So by all means recognise your own feelings, but rather than project a label – "revenge taker" – onto the child, remember NLP principle number 8: we all have our own map of reality. So the label comes out of your map. Step out of your own map and then, with principle number 8 in mind, hold your feelings to one side and look and listen to gain an insight into the *child's* mental map. Developing your own emotional intelligence in this way improves your personal resilience in the face of conflict and allows you to intervene more effectively. It is an easy skill to develop. For the student, emotional intelligence is more likely to develop, the more they are involved in directing and managing their own learning and the stresses that come with it. How good are you at picking up on these learning anxieties to prevent learning stress? Or at teaching pupils how to handle it, to become more emotionally aware and intelligent? As you look around the classroom, what are the clues and cues that you pick up on as the signs of unacceptable behaviour that need your intervention?

- Is it the physical arrangements and postures of the children?
- Is it the level, quality, tone and pitch of the conversations going on?
- Is it the "feel" of the room?

Young children may not have the vocabulary to articulate the emotions they feel, or what they think, particularly when they are at the edge of their understanding. "My tummy hurts 'cos he grabbed me around the neck," a young child once said in my class. He was describing his fear of the other boy. Fear and sadness often get described as a physical symptom such as not feeling well. For you, not feeling well may mean having a tummy ache. For the young child, it is not a physical sensation that is probably being identified, but an emotion. Careful questioning, appropriate language and skilful interpretation then become the keys to unravelling what lies behind their words – and, underneath them, the anxieties that give rise to their negative behaviour. The skill of formulating a question that unblocks the child's thinking, changes their mental maps, frees them from their self-imposed limitations is the essence of the art, craft and science of teaching.

The teacher as coach

"Our children need coaches not cheerleaders."
– Curry and Johnson, *Beyond Self Esteem*

How good are you at detecting learning anxiety and intervening to prevent learning stress? Do you distinguish between the sort of stress that closes the learning down and that stress which is necessary to provide the creative tension to make a learning leap? Equally important as knowing when to intervene is knowing when *not* to because that, too, can lower the learning stress that may be triggering the dysfunctional behaviour. Terri Apter (1997) has coined the phrase "emotional coaching" for her approach to decreasing learning stress and raising self-esteem. It emphasises the importance of gaining rapport through the adoption of a relevant physical posture and relationship to the child and the use of appropriate language. Apter's book is centred on the behavioural level of Dilts's neurological levels for the learner. At this level the complementary teacher role is that of coach.

In the commercial world, a whole new coaching profession has sprung up around the concept of getting the best from managers by helping them develop a healthy work–life balance. The key skill of these coaches is that of asking "powerful" questions – questions that prompt managers to reflect on their experience, their actions

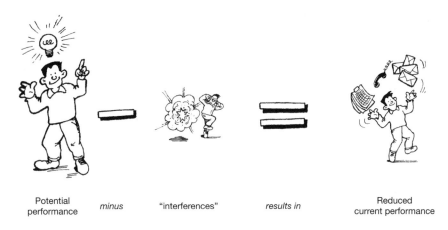

| Potential performance | minus | "interferences" | results in | Reduced current performance |

Figure 3.6: The diminishing of full potential

and their beliefs and values, to confront blocks and to take action to achieve what they want in their lives. There is a simple belief that says, "You are always more than you currently think you are." And there's a simple equation that coaches follow in aiding others achieve their goals. The belief and the equation (Figure 3.6) illustrate that what we do or achieve is very often much less than we could *potentially* do or achieve. Our true potential achievement gets diminished by "interferences". These interferences can be external, as Lozanov (1979) noticed (school and class norms, the physical environment etc.) but it is the internal ones (such as their own values and beliefs, the perception of their role in the classroom) that have their origins in the three anxieties that are more likely to be long-lasting. These are the sources of our self-imposed, limiting beliefs – the beliefs that are about the permission they give themselves to do something, to be capable of something, to become someone.

For your pupils in the classroom, they can be their beliefs and expectations about:

- The relevance of the outcomes of their task;
- Their perception of the inappropriateness of the task to themselves;
- Their own capability to do the task;
- Whether they even deserve to become more capable at the task.

You can see that to maintain or raise the self-esteem of an individual effectively (i.e., helping him achieve his full potential), it pays to know which of the three basic anxieties is likely to be most dominant for him. You can then speak directly to that anxiety, allay it and raise the child's perception of his worth. Anxieties and emotions can be contagious. So a good indicator of the child's latent anxiety is often your own emotional response to him, as you may intuitively pick up and reflect back his own anxiety. For example, if you feel a degree of threat or challenge or even anger, then it is possible that the child is someone wanting more control over his own development – a power seeker (to use one of Dreikurs's term). If you feel tired with the child or even slightly hurt by the continued misbehaviour, and you are reflecting that hurt, it may be because the child has constantly been seeking your or another's attention – he wants to be noticed as an individual who deserves care. You are picking up on this. If you feel irritated, frustrated or even apprehensive, you may be facing a child who has been unable to make the contribution he wished to make to the work and you are detecting that latent fear.

The coach and manager forge an alliance focused on the manager's learning – coach and manager contract to play their respective parts in making that alliance an effective learning one. To do that, the coach has to balance the tension that exists between your present and your future – between your dreams and aspirations – which is the stark reality of where you are right now. If that tension becomes high enough the relationship snaps and the balloon of your dreams disappears up in to the stratosphere, ensuring that your present situation rolls on to become your future also. If there is no tension, then there is no energy to motivate you forward to make the dream come true. Once again, you stay in your present state.

As a teacher, you work to help each learner balance this tension. It demands the ability to maintain the dignity of the learner, her belief in herself, her self-esteem, while helping her to face the reality of her present struggles without judgment or censure. It means acknowledging and recognising progress and achievement and not punishment and reward. As the actor Patrick Stewart noted about his own secondary modern school teachers, "If you behave as if people are smart, they will be smart." Maintaining the tension can be helped by keeping one eye on the other levels that stretch between the present and the future realities (see Figure 3.7).

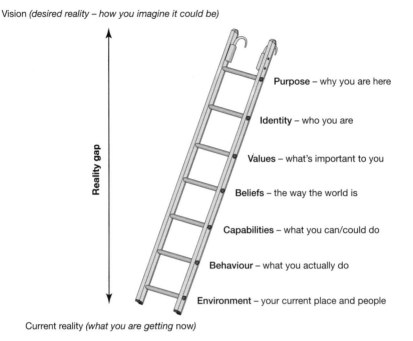

Vision *(desired reality – how you imagine it could be)*

Purpose – why you are here

Identity – who you are

Values – what's important to you

Beliefs – the way the world is

Capabilities – what you can/could do

Behaviour – what you actually do

Environment – your current place and people

Reality gap

Current reality *(what you are getting* now*)*

Figure 3.7: The motivational ladder

Putting Apter's emotional coaching ideas into practice means remembering that current behaviour is related to all the other levels and their corresponding teacher roles. One of the potentially exhausting aspects of teaching today is the rapid switching between these different roles, not just for one child but for many. No other profession or occupation has such a multiplicity of facets being switched off and on so many times per day. In today's classrooms, many teachers could benefit from having their own personal emotional coach!

There are two useful ways in which you can help children manage their emotions. The first is to teach them the skill of centring. The second is to reinforce that skill by talking to their unconscious mind by layering a trance-inducing script over the centring exercise. Examples of these are given in Part III.

Exercise 3.3: Which is your most likely approach to conflict?

Read through both the strengths and weaknesses tables and rate yourself according to how you answer the questions. This will give you a rough and ready profile of how you view your own emotional stance.

1. Not at all
2. Sometimes
3. Often
4. Very typical of me

Overdone to the point of weakness

Behavioural strengths

Collaborating	• Do you spend a lot of time in collaboration? *Not all confrontations need to have optimal resolutions – there is a limit to the effective use of time and energy.*
Rating _____	• Does your collaborative behaviour prompt reciprocal behaviour in the student? *If so, you may be missing some cues about the student's feelings, anxieties, needs and defensiveness.*
Compromising	Is compromise the dominant characteristic of your classroom confrontations? • Do you focus on the details of resolving the "here and now" situation, and lose sight of principles, values or longer-term objectives? • Do you find yourself a little too soft or sensitive to be effective in confrontations? *If so, you might find the climate limits the development of really good relationships.*
Rating _____	
Competing	• Is your "difficult" pupil reluctant to admit their uncertainties to you? *In a competitive climate, pupils will often act more assertively than they really feel to cloak their insecurity.*
Rating _____	• Is your student submissive, biddable, unadventurous, unforthcoming? *If so, perhaps it is because they have learned that it doesn't pay to disagree with you, or have given up trying to influence you.*

Avoiding	• Does the learning in your classroom suffer, because you don't resolve difficult behaviour sufficiently well?
Rating _____	*Key traits of good teachers from a pupil's point of view are fairness and consistency. There are two characteristics that are often lost though avoidance behaviours.*
Accommodating	• How often do you feel that you bend over backwards for the pupil, but they don't reciprocate?
	An easygoing nature is open to being seen as "soft" and taken advantage of.
Rating _____	• Would your colleagues consider your discipline "lax"?
	Discipline for its own sake is of little value, but often there are school norms that need to be maintained for a consistent approach to misbehaviour.

Behavioural weaknesses

Collaborating	• Do you find it difficult to see differences with a pupil as opportunities for mutual gain (see the NLP presuppositions)?
	All confrontations have the potential to be unproductive and energy-sapping. Repeated
Rating _____	*confrontations with the same person can install a sense of pessimism that shuts out the recognition of possibilities.*
	• Do pupils often fail to carry through the commitments they made in what seemed a resolution of a conflict?
	If so, it is often because their needs weren't actually being addressed in the "agreed" actions.
Compromising	• Do you find yourself too sympathetic to the needs of the pupils to be effective in confronting their behaviour?
	Teachers, generally, are in the profession
Rating _____	*because they care about pupils.*
	• Do you find it hard to make concessions?
	Sometimes your own insecurity prompts an overreliance on the rules or behaviour which is unbending and therefore dysfunctional.

Competing	• Do you sometimes feel powerless in confrontation?
	You may just be unskilled in the use of the positional power you have as a teacher – or uncomfortable using it!
	• Do you sometimes have trouble taking a firm stand?
Rating _____	*As in the compromise box above, the vocational sense of care for a pupil can sometimes override the need to take positive remedial action.*

Avoiding	• Do you find yourself decreasing the self esteem of a pupil?
	You may need to develop the skill of avoiding potentially disruptive situations.
Rating _____	• Do you often feel hassled or harried by a number of issues in your classroom?
	You may need to clarify priorities and see what is and is not important.

Accommodating	• Do you have difficulty maintaining the cooperation of certain pupils?
	• Do they see you as unreasonable?
Rating _____	*You may need to learn to accommodate them on minor areas to be strong on major ones.*

Results

Add the ratings for both the weaknesses and the strengths of each style and complete the bar chart below to show your profile.

	Strengths	Weaknesses	Total
Collaborating	_____	_____	_____
Compromising	_____	_____	_____
Competing	_____	_____	_____
Avoiding	_____	_____	_____
Accommodating	_____	_____	_____

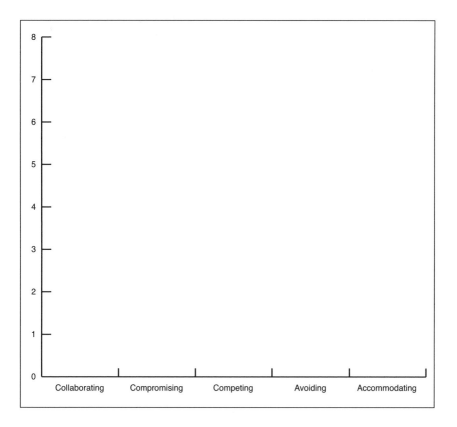

Key conclusions

- There is a range of theories about good behaviour management. There is no one right answer and most teachers use what works from all of them. The theories can make more sense, however, when applied as approaches at the appropriate neurological levels.
- Under stress, our social behaviour is usually shaped (distorted) by one of three anxieties linked to the defensive reactions of fight, flight or freeze.
- We all seem to have a "preferred" anxiety and subsequently a most likely way of dealing with any conflict – avoidance, accommodation, competition, compromise or collaboration.
- Our actual external achievement is often less than our truly highest inner potential.
- Coaching techniques are useful in helping children achieve that higher potential.

Sources and further reading for this chapter

Apter, T, 1997, *The Confident Child*, W W Norton, New York.

Balbernie, R, 1998, *Infant–Parent Psychotherapy and Infant Mental Health: A Strategy for Early Intervention and Prevention*, Severn NHS Trust, Gloucester.

Berliner, D, and Casanova, U, 1993, *Putting Research to Work in Your School*, SIRI/Skylight, Arlington Heights, IL.

Blackerby, D A, 1996, *Rediscover the Joy of Learning*, Success Skills, Oklahoma City, OK.

Canter, L, and Canter, M, 1992, *Assertive Discipline: Positive Behaviour Management for Today's Classroom*, Canter and Associates, Inc., Santa Monica, CA.

Csikszentmihalyi, M, 1996, *Creativity: Flow and the Psychology of Discovery and Invention*, HarperCollins, New York.

Curry, N E, and Johnson, C N, 1990, *Beyond Self Esteem*, The National Association for the Education of Young Children, Washington, D.C.

Dreikurs, Rudolf, *Child Guidance and Education collected papers*, 1984.

Elton, Lord, 1989, *Discipline in Schools*, Report of the Committee of Enquiry chaired by Lord Elton HMSO, London.

Glasser, W, 1998, *Choice Theory in the Classroom*, Harper Perennial, New York.

Heron, J, 1989, *The Facilitator's Handbook*, Kogan Page, London.

Hill, F, and Parsons, L, 2000, *Teamwork in the Management of Emotional Behavioural Difficulties*, David Fulton, London.

Le Doux, J, 1998, *The Emotional Brain*, Phoenix, London.

Lozanov, G, 1979, *Suggestology and Outlines of Suggestopedia*, Gordon and Breach Publishers, New York.

McDermot, I, and Jago, W, 2001, *The NLP Coach*, Piatkus, London.

Maines, B, and Robinson, G, 1991, *Teacher Talk*, Lucky Duck Publishing, Bristol.

Porter, L, 2000, *Behaviour in Schools: Theory and Practice for Teachers*, Open University Press, Buckinghamshire.

Rogers, W, 1994, *Behaviour Recovery: A Whole School Programme for Mainstream Schools*, Longman, Harlow, Essex.

Stewart, P, 2002, My Best Teacher, *Times Educational Supplement*, 29 March.

Part III

Just How Do I Do It?

Chapter Four
It's All in the Mind

"As you are reading these words, you are taking part in one of the wonders of the natural world. For you and I belong to a species with a remarkable ability: we can shape events in each other's brains with exquisite precision."

Steven Pinker, *The Language Instinct*

Pinker's words can be taken literally. By the words we use, we can stimulate the sensations and create pictures and sounds in another's mind – we call it communication. We can never fully know how well the representation in the other person's mind matches the images in our own mind that that we were trying to convey. Poor communicators obviously do not attain the precision that Pinker claims. However, the language approaches developed in NLP are some of the best tools available to help us achieve high levels of successful communication – both in conveying images and ideas and in understanding the mental maps of others. If you've come straight to this part of the book, it probably means that you already know consciously or unconsciously something about NLP and you want to put these ideas into practice.

Getting down to the nitty-gritty – the meta-model of language

 The meta-model of language is a classification of a dozen or more linguistic patterns that prevent clear and effective communication by obscuring the meaning behind what the speaker is saying. There are many commonly used words and sentence formations that indicate a no-go area of thinking for individuals, depending on the specific filters operating in their heads. The NLP communication model groups these into three types: deletions, generalisations and distortions (Figure 1.1).

115

Table 4.1: Meta-model examples

Language filter	Meta-model patterns
Deletions	**Simple deletions** Sentences that need a subject or an object to make complete sense *I'm fed up; She's a brighter pupil; they just don't care* **Unspecified verbs** Verbs that obscure the actual behaviour or sensory experience *He is so frustrating to teach* **Nominalisations** Verbs converted into nouns, actions treated as things *Communication is poor in this school* **Lack of referential index** Statements that need a specific subject to make complete sense *It's so boring here*
Generalisation	**Universals** Words that assume that a single event can be extended to all situations, or all times, to all people, etc. *He never smiles; it's always the same here; they're all useless at maths* **Possibilities** Statements that indicate that the speaker puts limits on their capabilities, choices and actions because of what they believe is possible *I wish I could draw; If only I could …I couldn't possibly …* **Necessities** Statements that assume an unwritten law, for the speaker and/or for everyone *I must be nice to him; you can't do what you want*
Distortions	**Mind reading** Stating as real, things that are imagined *He thinks I'm not up to it; I don't think she really likes me* **Lost performances** Value statements that omit who is doing the valuing or who is being judged *It's not good to argue in staff meetings* **Poor cause–effect links** Assumption that statement A leads directly to statement B with no proof *His 'couldn't care less' attitude makes me angry.* **False equivalences** Assumption that statement A is the same as a different statement, B *You haven't brought your book? You're so irresponsible* **Presuppositions** Unspoken assumptions behind the words, taken as true *It gets easier as you go along*

Bandler and Grinder refined and subdivided these filter patterns and then devised a set of corresponding questions to uncover the hidden meaning, thereby improving the dialogue between two people.

It is this classification that is known as the meta-model of language. It can be used to restructure a person's thinking so as to open up the former no-go areas where they indicate that the speaker holds certain assumptions or beliefs that limit his thinking and therefore his behaviour. Most teachers have already acquired a working knowledge of the meta-model's interrogative approach to getting beyond what a pupil first says. The model puts that intuitive learning onto a formal conceptual basis, which will allow you to become even more successful at helping students move beyond their mental blocks.

Getting below the surface of the language patterns to uncover these can liberate the person from the underpinning belief and increase their resourcefulness. This tool takes the speaker back down their "ladder of inferences" around the issue in question. The three steps in using this model are:

1. Recovering the important bits of information that have been left out or lost in generalisations;
2. Exploring the boundaries of the child's thinking;
3. Uncovering the meanings the child has attached to their experience.

The primary task is to take the child back to a behavioural or sensory-based description of what is being communicated and then use the information gained to push the boundaries out and reform the child's interpretation of their experience. To do this, Bandler and Grinder:

- Used the meta-model's "precision" questions to *discover unspoken facts*;
- *Challenged the unspoken assumptions* behind the words or expressions used;
- *Matched the vocabulary* used by the speaker to convey empathy and develop rapport;
- Sometimes deliberately mismatched the vocabulary to help *disrupt and then change* the person's mental picture of the events;

- *Checked* how things and events were connected in the person's mind;
- Often *used visualisation techniques* to open up the person's mental map.

The full structure of the categories with their sub-patterns is shown in Table 4.1. To become familiar with the patterns, start with yourself. Do any of the examples or processes sound familiar to you? Which ones can you hear yourself saying? Do you hear any specific ones used frequently in your classroom? Do you know someone who uses one or other of these linguistic patterns regularly? As you explore your own speech patterns and change them, you will appreciate the improvement in the behaviour of your pupils that follows.

Exercise 4.1: Using the meta-model

Begin to notice your own use of these speech patterns and which you use most often in everyday life. When you notice them, challenge them using the questions in Table 5.2.

- Notice the effect on you as you use these language shifts, and then notice how other people respond differently to them.

- Achieve even bigger shifts in your own behaviour and the way you look at issues by applying them to your internal self-talk – those things you say to yourself when in an emotional or anxious state.

- How often do you use words such as "must", "have to", "should" etc., when talking about your own behaviour or capabilities?

Presuppositions

A key understanding of the meta-model is the power of the unspoken assumptions that lie behind your language. All communication is only partial. What the listener constructs from what has been said is often an approximation to what the speaker intended. These implied assumptions, which are usually taken as true by the listener, are known as *presuppositions* and depend very much on the form of what was actually said.

"Jane and I had a wonderful weekend" presupposes:

(1) That there is someone called Jane;

(2) That the speaker spent the weekend with her;

(3) They did something together that gave them pleasure.

Detecting presuppositions – and particularly in managing behaviour – is the a key communication skill.

This often comes down to seeing certain words as parcels that have to be carefully unwrapped to find their meaning. For example, what does "wonderful" mean here?

The National Literacy Programme in the UK has raised teachers' knowledge of the structure of grammar and so all teachers now know that the basic sentence structure has the form of subject, verb, object, and usually contain a selection of nouns and verbs. Nouns *presuppose* that something exists and is named; verbs presuppose that some action is taking, or has taken, place. In some sentences the subject or the object is missing or poorly defined. Their existence has to be presupposed by the listener.

The careful use of presuppositions is a particularly powerful way of influencing a child's limiting beliefs to move them to more empowering ones. In the classroom, the most useful are presuppositions about time – presupposing that the current problem is already in the past: "Graphs always appear strange when you first do them, and ... it was most difficult for you then ... when you tried the first few ... and I suppose you have found other things difficult before graphs, so ..." Then they presuppose a future change will happen: "I wonder how many more examples of graphs you will do before you feel good about knowing that ... you can do them"; or "I don't know when you'll be able to do these graphs ... maybe now ... or by the end of the lesson, or tomorrow ... and it doesn't really matter when ... you can do them soon."

Sometimes, deliberately mixing the tenses in the same sentence helps to shift the problem into the past and create the impression that it has now been resolved satisfactorily: "I see that that is a problem, wasn't it?"

The more complex the mix, the more the conscious mind gets tied up and the more the unconscious mind hears the hidden message: "Just think ... what it will be like at the end of the year when ... you can learn that now ... and then ... look back at this section on graphs and see what it felt like then to have had that problem ... as you think about it now ..."

The deliberate and subtle use of presuppositions in your own language will help you modify another person's beliefs and subsequently their behaviour. So, when you begin to make more use of presuppositions, then you will be a better behaviour manager.

Nominalisations

A second appreciation underpinning the use of the meta-model is that very often we use abstract nouns or labels that disguise the underlying behaviour and sensory data. These occur when a behaviour described by a verb gets converted into a noun; when an action gets converted into a pseudo "thing" or object. There is for example no concrete object called a "communication". This noun has been grown from the behaviour of two people communicating. The making of such nominalisations then spawns many presuppositions. How often have you heard someone moan, "Communication is really poor in this school"? It omits just who is not communicating with whom – which is what you really need to know. This combination of nominalisations and presuppositions makes it more difficult to improve how the people in the school communicate with each other. The questions in the table help penetrate this fog to reveal the behaviours that are actually being complained about. Deploying such questions is often the first step in moving to improve a difficulty. A greater level of miscommunication occurs when the nominalisations are evaluative or judgmental: "You are just stupid!" Apart from committing the cardinal sin for any teacher – that of attacking at an identity level, rather than at the behavioural one – the word "stupid" here is probably being used as a huge generalisation of a number of behaviours or actions. The speaker has lumped them together under this label and then pinned it on the listener. Behaviourally, a child can do nothing positive or go anywhere constructively with this label. It does nothing to promote changed behaviour. Cutting through such labels to get at the concrete behaviour, and offering feedback on this, is the only way forward. The meta-model is a powerful tool for doing just that.

Developing the "Merlin" in you – hypnotic language approaches

 The Milton model of language is the NLP approach that creates representations in the other person's mind, where you do not need to know the precise details of the images, sounds or feelings being generated. This way, since the listener is supplying the detail, he is creating a really meaningful representation for himself – although he thinks that you somehow know what he's seeing, hearing or feeling. In other words it turns the meta-model on its head and uses it to effect change. Fortune-tellers are skilled at making statements or asking questions that have just the right balance between vagueness and detail, between fact and guesswork, for you to attach significance to what they are saying. Without realising it, you fill in the details around their generalisations and then are led to think that they have the uncanny knack of knowing something that they could not possibly have known any other way than through their mystic powers.

The case for obscurity

On thoughts and words 1
If no thought
your mind does visit,
make your speech
not too explicit.

© Piet Hein Groks, 'The Case for Obscurity', *Collected Grooks 1*, p. 43, reprinted with the permission of Piet Hein, a/s DK-5500 Middelfart, Denmark

Bandler and Grinder found that one of the therapists they studied, Milton Erickson, was excellent at getting rapport with his subjects, but seemed to do so in a similar way to that in which fortune-tellers approach their clients. He used many abstract words and nominalised verbs. That is, he had perfected a very convincing way of speaking that seemed to say much without saying anything too specific. Piet Hein's little grook suggests it is way to cover up your own lack of ideas, but Erickson used it positively as an effective therapeutic intervention. Highly nonspecific language forces you to go into your own mental world to find experiences and beliefs that you can associate with the words you are hearing. Searching in your own mind and scanning your memories while someone talks to you is a form of trance very similar to daydreaming. Because nothing too specific is being said, nothing in what is being said to you can be directly contradicted. More importantly, by making your own sense of the words, the speaker (therapist or fortune-teller!) seems to be talking sense and a high level of rapport is created between you. This technique of deliberately speaking in a vague and generalised way is now a standard approach used by hypnotherapists. As an example, if I had used this in the introduction to this book I might have said something like:

> I know you are wondering how easy it is use these patterns in the normal course of the day in school. What's good about your wondering is that, because your consciously aware mind is processing these ideas, your unconscious mind will already be learning them. And you probably know more about them at an unconscious level than you think you do, don't you? Everyone learns in this way, so you should find that, even while you are reading this book, and thinking about these ideas, the concepts are being assimilated into your understanding. Successful assimilation means that they will come naturally to you when you need them. So … as you sit here reading this book, are you conscious of the pressure of your seat on your back and all the time hearing the sounds around you, you wonder what … you are learning right now … and you are learning, are you not? And you will be pleasantly surprised at how much you have learned already about vague language and you have learned it … maybe not only in your conscious mind, but also in your unconscious mind … and you are unconscious, aren't you? And you … don't … mind. Whether you realise this now or later, when you find yourself using these ideas in the classroom, is less important. The fact that you can use them will result in a happier, more productive classroom, won't it?

Now, what specifically has been said? Very little. But did you notice what images, thoughts, memories came into your mind as you read it?

Bandler and Grinder soon realised that what Milton Erickson was doing was the exact opposite of the meta-model in that he was deliberately using speech patterns to delete, distort and generalise. Such communication seemed to be very effective in getting the client both to follow Erickson's suggestions and to resolve their own problems. He was using Lozanov's idea of split-level communication. For teachers, these two outcomes can also be the main benefits of inducing an "everyday" sort of hypnotic trance (akin to that which we sometimes experience while driving or jogging) in pupils. It might seem to go against the grain of the whole training and practice of most teachers to believe that there is advantage in promoting daydreaming or a sort of absent-mindedness among their students. It doesn't appear common sense, yet with a little reflection we know that it is precisely from this state that many scientific discoveries and inventions have sprung.

Another skill of Erickson's was the ability to utilise quickly anything unexpected and incorporate it smoothly into what he was saying at the time, so that it seemed planned. All good teachers of science acquire this skill early in their careers as their demonstration experiments refuse to work as planned! And all teachers know how to make best use of "happenstance", even when it is potentially disruptive, such as a police siren or the first fall of snow.

In Chapter Three, I drew your attention to the right and left hemispheres of the brain and the different ways in which they seem to process the incoming sensory information. Milton Erickson's approach used the fact that the right hemisphere understands simple messages, bypassing the left hemisphere, and can therefore be communicated with, directly. He did this by enclosing a "right-brain" message within a normal-sounding sentence, marking it out through changes in vocal tone or emphasis. It is the acoustic equivalent of using capitals in writing. As you THINK about all THIS and read the sentence OUT you will use language more CAREFULLY. While the left hemisphere is operating on the full sentence, the right hemisphere hears "think this out carefully".

Erickson made this sort of language more effective by tying up the left hemisphere in logical puzzles. "Do you believe that BY reading THIS BOOK NOW, you will be a better teacher?" If you were hearing this spoken rather than seeing it written, in the right context, your brain would now be now faced with a problem about the possible confusion resulting from an ambiguity in understanding in the form of by/buy. Both words sound the same but the left brain has to work on deciding which is the one needed here. While it is working sequentially and logically to choose the word "by" for the complete set of words in the sentence to make sense, the right hemisphere has heard the four tonally marked or otherwise emphasised words. It could choose, therefore, "buy" as the most sense-making word in the sentence "buy this book now". A subliminal message that perhaps I should have put on this book's cover! In this way Erickson embedded many instructions or commands to his clients within his vague, seemingly rambling, talk. His way of speaking – its speed and its tonal changes – probably also helped stimulate alpha brain rhythms, which promote that relaxed, creative state described in Chapter Three. This allows the person to tap into their own unconscious strengths and as a result become more resourceful in how they tackle their issues.

Another technique that Erickson used to divert the conscious, sequence-processing mind was to use sentences containing multiple negatives. And I don't know whether or not you've not yet thought of using many negatives, or not even one or two, in your conversations with pupils. Don't you think you can do this? Honestly, you can. The stream of negatives becomes confusing, forcing listeners inwards to make sense of what they are hearing, thereby losing awareness of other things that are being said. Erickson used this short lapse in learners' concentration to give them an embedded command – an instruction that will have been heard by the unconscious mind, but not be remembered consciously. This is a form of "posthypnotic" suggestion – something a person may later act on without directly appreciating the source of the stimulus for the behaviour.

Hypnosis is based on the belief that it is possible to connect with the mental processes operating below the threshold of your everyday conscious awareness, while your conscious mind is diverted to other tasks. In the paragraph above, "command" is perhaps too strong a word to use, because no one can command you to do what you do not wish to do, whether you're hypnotised or not. However, there is some research evidence that a lot of the information received by the unconscious mind is not just received but is also processed there, outside your conscious awareness. And it is thought that this processing can subtly affect your subsequent behaviour. This is the basis for the concept of posthypnotic suggestion, which was what Erickson was very skilful at using with clients.

Bandler and Grinder took all these ideas and utilised them in gaining greater rapport with their trainees, to accelerate the learning of the material they were presenting and to promote the behaviours they were looking to develop. I am not sure, as a teacher, how the use of these techniques has the potential to alter the learning conditions in your own classroom, but I am sure you can use them effectively to help pupils to change their behaviour in ways that benefit them. And as with all new ideas, sometimes it is just important to give it a go in the classroom.

Storytelling and metaphoric language

"Metaphors are made in the unconscious and something in the metaphor-making process itself is resistant to conscious examination and analysis."

– Nigel Lewis, *The Book of Babel*

I explained a little of the power of metaphoric speech in Chapter Two. When struggling to resolve a problem, we have been taught to approach it rationally and consciously. That usually means we take an inductive or a deductive path to the solution – we either start from some general principle or understanding of how the world works and apply it to the experience to produce some new insight, or we gather all the specific data we can around the experience and synthesise them upwards to form an answer. One is a movement up the logical levels from the specific to the general and the other is a movement down from the general to the specific. All of us may feel more capable at the one process than we do at the other and so we tend to lean towards one side of McCarthy's 4-MAT (Figure 1.5, page 19) learning diagram than the other. And for much of the time one or other of these movements will produce an answer. But when they don't, when we get stuck, we need a different approach.

What Edward de Bono (1982) and other people encouraged some decades ago was a breakaway from these up/down problem-solving movements into a sideways one – what he termed lateral thinking. Describing the problem metaphorically is the most powerful way of prompting lateral thinking and the search for alternative, more creative ways through an apparent impasse, because it engages the unconscious part of your mind. Telling stories, using metaphors and analogies, helps you to describe what you know inside, instinctively; what, up to that point, you have been unable to find the right words for. The metaphors can be either direct or indirect. They can have a 1:1 correspondence with the situation or they can be more far more subtle and diverse. The first tends to be useful in more closed-ended situations, where you want to guide a student to a known or desired conclusion; the second, in an open-ended case, where you want the student to explore many different possible avenues and end points.

Behaviour change as a journey from the present state to the desired one is a common metaphor for devising an action plan that works. Seeing it as a motocross event or a car rally, you can get the child to answer such route-planning questions as:

- Where am I now? What is my start point? (Describe the current behaviours.)
- Where do I want to end up? (Describe desired state/behaviours.)
- What route shall I take? (What actions do I need to undertake?)
- What do I need to get there? (What skills, knowledge do I need?)
- How do I know whether I am still on course? (Establish checkpoint.)
- Am I on schedule? (How fast can I travel, what are the target times for each stage?)

You will choose your own metaphors and stories to get the outcome you desire. They need not be complete stories – our everyday figures of speech can be equally powerful. How often do we use such turns of phrase as "a steep learning curve", "up a blind alley", "stuck in a rut" in the classroom?

Do you think you can develop an extensive range of such metaphors, analogies and expressions that could help in behaviour management? Practise them in the classroom and notice which ones are most effective. You will recognise their power in the response of the student – a change in physiology, an intake of breath, a light dawning in the facial expression, a shift in emotional state. This is a skill that definitely improves with practice so that you can create or choose the most effective metaphor for the situation.

Shaped daydreaming or state-inducing talk

You can put both these two "hypnotic" speech patterns together by telling a story that is couched in Ericksonian language. This is a particularly powerful way of using the imagination to produce a state of mind that is emotionally supportive of, and prepared for, new learning. Talk, and particularly guided-visualisation talk, is one way of creating the mental and emotional conditions for learning associated with the brain's alpha rhythms. A guided visualisation is an "in-trancing" way of telling a story to create mind pictures and elicit emotional states. It helps generate the alpha rhythms in the brain that are necessary for that state of relaxed alertness to optimise learning. For younger children, the process is similar to daydreaming, but daydreaming with a purpose and a shape. Such visualisation is a powerful way of changing negative thoughts and emotions into positive ones. It can also be a mental rehearsal of the learning that is to follow by opening up the children's minds to new possibilities, new skills, and new capabilities. This is often described as "pathwalking". Here are the basic steps:

1. Get the pupil to relax in order to close down conscious thoughts (the beta rhythms). This is enhanced by the use of background mood music such as classical baroque, particularly those pieces that have a beat of sixty to the minute (e.g., Pachelbel's *Canon*, Mozart's "Romane" from *Eine Kleine Nachtmusik*, Albinoni's *Adagio*), or African trance music, which, at eight tone pulses per second, is close to that of the normal alpha rhythms of the brain's relaxed state.

2. Next, lead the pupil to think of the behavioural issue, by *picturing* a situation, and to *talk* through what is happening

around her, how others are reacting and talking, and how she *feels* (that is, prompt the use of all three key sensory modalities).

3. Then develop the picture to where the issue is resolved. What is happening now? What is different in the responses of the people around the pupil? How differently does she feel?

4. Future-pace her learning. That is, get her to imagine a time in the near future when she is likely to use the new learning and see herself deploying the knowledge or skills.

Sometimes, when it is a learning block that is prompting the misbehaviour, pupils may find it difficult to articulate or express. This is particularly so with younger children. Young or old, child or adult, it helps in these cases to engage the right-brain approach and ask the person to describe it in sensory terms:

- If the block has a shape, what does it look like? Or what colour is it?
- If it could make a noise or talk, what would it sound like, or say?
- How does it feel? How do you feel? How do you feel about the way it makes you feel?

Pictorial descriptions are good because you can create solutions with other pictures – ravines can be bridged, brick walls can be scaled by ladders and so on. Also, if you have already detected the child's preferred modality for acquiring information, telling the story using the other, less preferred, modalities can help bypass her normal, conscious mind and processing patterns, and therefore may open up alternative choices to her. If you have never used these approaches, then, as you read about them now, what is *your* reaction? If you think it sounds unrealistic, then that is probably your left-brain thinking pattern kicking in (although it may be accompanied by some right-brain stuff involving pies in the sky, or pigs with wings!). All I can say is: don't just believe it – experiment with it. It gets easier the more you do it, and the results can be quite extraordinary.

Stories in quotations

Richard Bandler asserts that you can say something that may be unacceptable to the pupil, if you embed it in a story about somebody else. How many times have you had a child use this ploy on you? How many times have you had a student approach you and ask for advice about a problem that "my friend" has? You can talk to the unconscious mind by telling a story in which you quote what someone else has reportedly said to you. The piece in the inner quotations is what you want the listener to hear in his unconscious mind:

> "I remember my own teacher telling me when I was in her class about another pupil she'd once had who thought that he'd never manage to draw graphs properly ... and she said to me, 'Listen carefully' ... and then she told me that she had said to him, 'You're confused right now about doing graphs and ... that's OK ... for now ... and I don't suppose ... you can imagine doing them well.' And I thought, 'Just like me!' Then she said that she said to this boy, 'Soon, you'll ... look back on this chat ... and wonder ... where the problem has gone and then you can relax.' And I know now she was right ... I ... don't ... know why I have told you that. Anyway ..."

One of the reasons for the enduring attraction of the tales of *The Arabian Nights* may be that it has this same structure of telling stories within stories, together with good examples of Milton Erickson's hidden commands. It obviously worked for Shahrazad in *The Arabian Nights*. One of her stories is really four tales nested one inside another and leads to the wonderfully disorienting (to the conscious mind, trying to keep track of it all) sequence:

Shahrazad said, "I heard O happy King,
   that the tailor told the king of China,
      that the beggar told the guests
         that he said to the caliph ..."

And then comes the central message of innocent people sentenced to death, which is surrounded by an outer message of forgiveness and reward for all concerned. Just the behaviours she wanted the king to exhibit towards her. And we all know that, for her, words really did work!

Words that change the internal mindscape – other linguistic approaches

Sleight of mouth

The Arbinger Institute (2000) described a common phenomenon in large organisations as "thinking in a box" and linked its source to the ease with which people fall into ways of behaving stemming from some form of self-deception. In the NLP model of communication, our beliefs, values and attitudes are thought of as shaping the distorting, deleting and generalising filters we deploy to process our daily experience. This results in our own personal mental map, our own perception of what is real and what is not – in other words, our own personal "box". One of the NLP principles suggests that there is no absolute reality. We manage our daily relationships in any one community or culture because of the degree of commonality between our individual maps. Our different boxes have many features in common.

Problems arise when the boxes are different. Insisting that our own box is the one and only reality is what the institute defined as self-deception. I believe only you can climb out of your own thinking and behaving box. (Just by stating this belief, you learn a little about my own personal box!) However, I also believe that it is possible to prompt a student to reconsider their own mental map, their own box, by carefully chosen words. After all, extending and deepening the mental maps of our students is the prime goal of teaching and the reason that children are put into years of compulsory schooling.

Researchers have analysed and classified the many different verbal ways teachers use to change students' mental maps. Robert Dilts dubbed them *sleight-of-mouth patterns*. This term was coined to illustrate the analogy of the stage magician's sleight of hand with this linguistic strategy. The technique is to redirect the speaker's attention while seemingly focusing on the content of what was just said. With a knowledge of the meta-model and the ability to challenge the deletions, distortions and generalisations that most of us use in everyday conversation, it is possible to alter the mental maps supporting the speaker's original statement. It consists of staying with the statement made, whilst placing it into a different context or

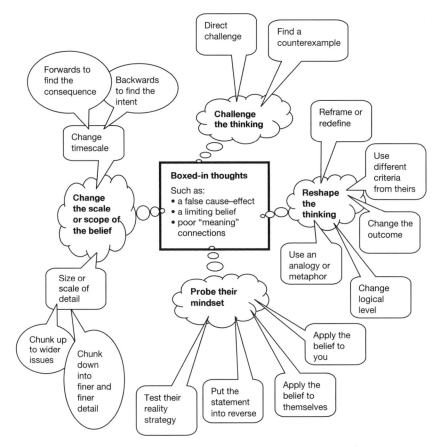

Figure 4.1: Sleight of mouth – strategies for breaking out of the box

frame of reference. When this is done skilfully, the student does not notice the movement of the background context and just accepts it. Often, the speaker's feelings, beliefs, attitudes or behaviour will then shift to match the new context.

All teachers have used one or more of these patterns intuitively at one time or another in trying to persuade, reason with or motivate a student. The meta-model classifies and extends these patterns, and allows you to use them with more subtlety and greater effectiveness. Examples of the different categories of possible responses to a typical statement will be found in Chapter Five. They are intended to help the student appreciate the limitations of their behaviour and to open up the possibility of alternative behaviours – alternatives to which their habitual thinking blinds them. With the framing of alternatives comes the possibility of choice, allowing students to opt for alternative ways of meeting their needs through a more socially acceptable and personally beneficial behaviour.

Verbal aikido and fogging

This is a linguistic device analogous to the martial art of aikido – "the way of blending energy". The founder of aikido, Ueshiba Morihe, said, "Aikido is not a technique to fight with or to defeat the enemy. It is a way to reconcile the world and to make human beings one family." In this Japanese self-defence method, the key principle is not to oppose the adversary's attack but to use its energy, add yours to it and then redirect it away from yourself. Students of aikido are taught to accept (and even embrace!) the attack, to come alongside and link with it, to understand better the attacker's position. William Rogers sums up this process as (1) relax, (2) tune in, (3) redirect.

In conflict management, the linguistic analogy is achieved by softening the verbal attack through agreement, wholly or in part, with what has just been said, and then adding your own redirecting commands. This technique is particularly suitable with children, because accepting the attack without judgment respects it. This allows you to gain more information about the child's stance, which improves your chances of redirecting their energy in a more positive direction.

Examples

- "I was only ..." ("Maybe you were, and yet ..." – A semi-agreement softener.)
- "You're being unfair ..." ("Yes, sometimes I may appear unfair and ..." – A more affirmative softener.)
- "You're picking on me!" ("Perhaps I do pick on you at times, but I still need you to ...")
- "It's boring!" ("Yes, you may think it boring to ... and yet ...")
- "I'm not the only one." ("Maybe, you're not the only one who has been out of his seat ...")

- "I don't like it there." ("Yes, you're probably right, you don't like moving, and yet …")
- "You're picking on me." ("Sometimes, I may pick on you … but right now …")
- "You are [any general name calling]." ("There may be some truth in that. I'm not perfect. What specifically is the problem?")

A variation on this approach is to use conditional statements after the initial agreement softener:

- "You're picking on me" ("Maybe, and if you … then you …")
- "I don't like it there." ("Yes, and when you've … then you can …")

Motivational talk

What are the skills of good influencers and negotiators? The key skill of such people is their ability to detect and understand the values and motivators of the other person. Building on what you have already learned from the previous parts of this book, you will know that language that can heighten motivation has the following elements:

- It has appropriate tonality (i.e., matched to the learner's)
- It uses the learner's favourite predicates ("You will soon get a good grasp of this skateboarding …")
- It uses possibility words rather than necessity ("If you can stick with it while you keep your head held up …")
- It contains a future description of the desired goal ("… until you'll find yourself balancing and rolling along without thinking …")
- It speaks to their uppermost anxiety ("Then you'll know you'll be one of the gang …")
- It has mixed away/towards elements (in that order) ("And, instead of staying here, you'll be able to go to the park with them …").

Another way of improving motivation is to base the structure of your conversation on the known meta-programs of the pupil. For instance, many children who have an away-from tendency will give you negative goals when you ask them what they want to ımplish – they tell you what they *don't* want. You will need to ʒert them into positive goals by such devices as: "… and if you weren't X-ing, what would you be doing?", "Instead of Y, what would you want?"

"I don't know" responses can be met with "I know you don't know, but, if you *did* know, what would it be?" This, surprisingly often, produces an answer.

Reframing

Reframing is a process of putting a different meaning to a specific event – a positive restructuring of the person's mind map. Everyone is familiar with the beer-glass question: "Is it half empty or half full?" It depends on your viewpoint. We have become used to hearing the problems facing education described as challenges. This is a simple reframe that could be thought of as mere political spin. Spin or not, the attitudes, mindset and motivation in tackling a challenge are quite different from those viewing the situation as a problem.

Just think about reframing personal attribute labels: "You're stubborn – while I'm persistent"; "You're rude – while I speak my mind openly"; "You're a busybody – while I'm concerned and thoughtful of others". We know that these "weaknesses" in others (and ourselves) are often just the other side of the coin of our strengths. So, with behaviour management, there is much to be gained in reframing the way we label a child's behaviour and in helping the child reframe the situation. Changing a child's viewpoint by talking to them has long been an unconscious skill of the good teacher. I am just making you aware of it, consciously, now, as one of the most powerful of skills in behaviour management. At a deeper level, it is a key skill in differentiating between the observed behaviour of the child and the unspoken intention behind it. This recognises that behaviour is a mode of communication and that hearing its message clearly is an important skill. The skill begins with asking the question, "What is this behaviour telling me?" A more powerful form of reframing is not just to reframe the words heard on the surface, but also to capture the positive intention. This form of reframing:

- Reflects the intended meaning of the student;
- Helps the student feel heard and understood;
- Can assist the student articulate and clarify the anxiety they want to express, that they are trying to express through their behaviour.

This is known as constructive reframing, and when used well, tells the student that you have reached the anxiety behind the words, that you understand their motivation. It is also another softening approach to what may have been said. In behaviour management, the process of reframing is even more powerful when embedded in the process of:

1. *Neutralising both the problem and/or any blame*
Statement: He's always swearing at me.
Reframe: You don't like the way he talks to you.
Statement: He's always interrupting me.
Reframe: You want to be able to work without disturbance.

2. *Reframing any derogatory remarks*
Statement: He must be stupid, because he keeps on ignoring me.
Reframe: You want him to take notice of what you're asking and you feel frustrated that things aren't any better.

3. *Changing negative goals to positive ones (or vice-versa, depending on the meta-program!)*
Statement: I don't want him sitting near me.
Reframe: So you want to find somewhere quiet to work.

The language of choice

> "What choice theory teaches is that everything we do is initiated by a satisfying picture of that activity that we store in our heads as a pleasant memory."
> – William Glasser, *Choice Theory in the Classroom*

Posing questions of choice for a child is an effective way of developing responsibility and improving behaviour. William Glasser's premise is that all our behaviour stems from choices (conscious or unconscious) that we make, and that we make the best choice of behaviour we believe available to us at the time (this is the same as the third NLP principle of Chapter One). His guide to choice making as a behaviour-management process emphasises the importance of getting pupils to develop the mindset that sees their behaviour as an active choice that they make and something over which they have control. This is also related to "thinking out of the box".

Knowing what we now know about sensory modalities, we might extend Glasser's description beyond pictures, to cover sounds, feelings and self-talk. Children's life experiences help them formulate the volitional meta-programs also described in Chapter One. There I said that choice changes the neurochemistry of the brain. If this is true, it means that you can help the child abandon old neural pathways by creating new ones and then reinforcing them, so that the old ones atrophy. This is the basis of the "catch them doing good" adage.

Remember that habits in the ways of relating to others stem from a choice made some time earlier in life – the child's best choice of behaviour to satisfy the need. If it met the child's need, then the behaviour is repeated. If successful a second time, the behaviour is deployed repeatedly, even when it is socially dysfunctional. It is abandoned only when it ceases to satisfy the driving need. Even then, it may not cease, as the habit has become a way of life and the original need lost in the mists of time. It may still be there, but not able to be articulated, having been covered over by many layers of beliefs about one's identity and about the world.

Changing such behaviour is dependent on getting clear, timely feedback on its inappropriateness or its failure to meet the need, and then guidance on alternative ways of fulfilling that need. Both the meta-model of language and the Milton model are designed to help this process happen by moving the child to be in a position of choice in his life. Gerard Gordon suggests you always point out the consequences of any behavioural choice and help students find an alternative behaviour that can meet their unspoken needs and which is not at your expense or that of fellow pupils. In the micro-climate of the classroom, this would be to adopt a more ecologically sound behaviour.

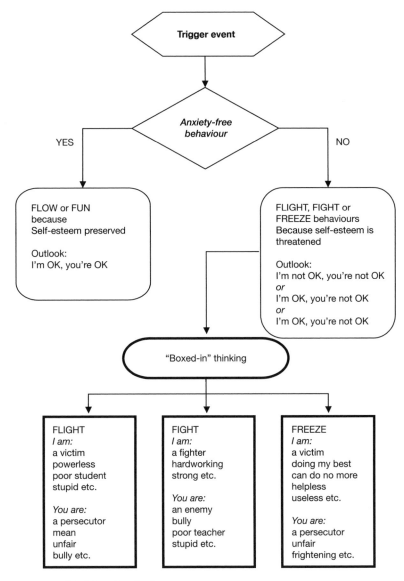

Figure 4.2: Thinking in the box

Gordon describes what he calls his behaviour-management approach as "choice-driven teaching". "Jane, where will you put those sweets, back in your pocket or on my desk?" is likely to be far more effective at getting Jane to stop eating her sweets than a direct order to put them away (which, if ignored, increases the indiscipline stakes) or confiscation (which leaves a negative emotional after effect). This particular example also contains a presupposition. The teacher is presupposing the action he wants to see – that the child will put the sweets away. The only choice is whether it is to be either in Jane's own safekeeping or that of the teacher! If Jane doesn't appreciate the consequences, they can be made very clear to her: "In your pocket means you will be able to eat them at playtime; on my desk means you'll not get them back until home time." By offering different choices and their related consequences you will be attempting to change the data filters at the bottom of Senge's ladder of inference (Figure 1.4) to get to new more needs-satisfying behaviours.

I observed a good example of a teacher using both presuppositions (from the meta-model techniques) and embedded commands (from the Milton model) in an exchange with a latecomer to her group, to open up the idea of choice. She was a behaviour-support teacher who was extracting a small group of nine-year-olds from their main classroom to work with her on their behaviour. As she introduced the group to a circle-time activity, a boy came bursting into the room and blurted out that he had been sent to join the group as he was "a little monkey". The teacher smiled and said to him, "That's really interesting. When did you decide to be a monkey?" (The question presupposed that to be a monkey was a choice he had made at some point.) The boy stopped talking to begin thinking about the question and particularly about the "when".

"I don't know," he eventually said. "Everyone just calls me a little monkey."

"But if you did know, when?" persisted the teacher. (As happened in this case, this question brings an answer surprisingly often.)

"My nan used to call me it when I was little," he volunteered, "and now everyone does."

"Aah," said the teacher, "so that's when you chose to be a monkey." The boy nodded. "So I suppose you can choose to be a different animal, can't you? Anyone you want to choose?"

The boy laughed and nodded agreement.

Exercise 4.2: Breaking out of the box

One way of examining the walls of your own box is to reverse your assumptions. First, just write down three adjectives that you might be likely to use when talking about a range of people. You can choose your own but here are some suggestions to get you started:

Education advisers are often …   Most pupils who cause trouble are …

_____   _____

_____   _____

_____   _____

Educationally, girls are often …   Educationally, boys are often …

_____   _____

_____   _____

_____   _____

Look back at what you have written and think about where these descriptors came from. Are they based on your beliefs? Do you have evidence to support your use of these generalisations? Are they based on what you read in the press or what you hear around you in the staffroom?

If these descriptors are ones that lurk in the background of your mind as you engage with pupils, how might they restrict your ability to respond flexibly to misbehaviour?

Now repeat the exercise, replacing your words with their polar opposites. What do you notice?

By considering your own mental map in this way, you may be better able to change its nature to one that enables you to be a better manager of behaviour in your classroom.

The teacher went on: "I have a pet rabbit at home called Pushkin. Do you think you can choose to be a rabbit like him, right now?"

"Course I can," replied the boy. "I can choose to be anything – what's he like?"

"You're right," said the teacher, "and Pushkin is big and brown-eyed and likes to sit quietly in the middle of my garden while watching everything going on around him. And if I do anything in the garden, he likes to join in. And if you were to be a rabbit like him now you'd know what to do, wouldn't you?"

"Of course," said the boy and he took up a chair and quietly joined the group – and remained well behaved for the rest of the session. At the end of the session, he smiled as the teacher commended him on his behaviour. As he left the room, turning around, he broke into a grin and said, "Next week, I might choose to be a lion!" After he had left, the teacher smiled wryly at me and said, "Well, he's learned the skill of making choices – next week he might have to learn about consequences!"

You can strengthen the choice–consequence chain by offering what is essentially a "single-bind" statement – one that links one effect to one cause, using comparatives. "The more you 'X', the less you 'Y' " or "The more you 'X', the more you 'Y' " – "The more time you spend playing now, the less free-choice time at the end of the week."

The next step is the language of no choice – double binds. These are questions that seem to offer a choice of behaviour, but actually contain no option about the behaviour and are an instruction to the pupil. Milton Erickson is often quoted as saying that he believed his clients should be perfectly free to do what he told them to do! "Do you want to do that now or later?" presupposes that the "that" will be done – the choice presented is only a superficial one, about *when* it will be done.

NVC – nonviolent communication

Nonviolent communication (NVC) is a methodology for addressing conflict that was developed by Marshal Rosenberg. It is designed to improve the communication between two people so that their conflict can be resolved to the satisfaction of both parties with no leftover resentment to act as the seed crystal for the next outbreak of hostility. The primary linguistic technique is to refrain from making evaluative remarks. In NLP terms, it emphasises the use of purely behavioural or sensory-specific language only in the transactions between the two people.

Judging and evaluating are processes common to everyone. Combined with the other that human tendency to categorise and pigeonhole people and events, they are very evident in everyday speech. Unpicking these patterns demands a knowledge of the meta-model of language (see beginning of this chapter) and the linguistic skills to employ it. It is a simple, effective technique that promotes the flow of information necessary to resolve differences, without leaving negative emotions or resentment in its wake. It provides a way of influencing people that improves rapport and helps restore good relationships. It works towards a better understanding of the other person and also emphasises personal responsibility for our behavioural choices and therefore their consequences. Nonviolent communication includes the ability to:

- Make clear, "clean" (i.e., non-evaluative) observations about what conflicts with your values;
- Evaluate honestly without losing rapport;
- Assertively request cooperation without sounding demanding or threatening;
- Empathise with the feelings and underlying anxieties or needs of the pupil.

The process recognises and identifies that most of us are programmed from an early age to speak what NVC characterises as evaluative language We often tend to label people and events mostly in a critical, judgmental and often combative way. We instinctively make values and/or moral judgments and nominalise behaviours. In our tone or manner we send the message this is "right or wrong", "good or bad", "normal or abnormal", "black or white". This starts the spiral of the breakdown of rapport and communication and leads to conflict. Appreciating that we use (and often need) labels to communicate complex ideas swiftly, we do have to be alert to the labels we hang around the necks of our students and to the effects they have on their self-esteem. The NVC approach helps pupils to become aware that we are often using labels and that these may be a barrier to clear communication. It can raise our awareness of alternative ways of speaking to each other.

Nonviolent communication works by using a "receiver-based" language. That is, vocabulary and sentence construction based on empathic listening that helps maintain rapport or regain it after it has disappeared in a confrontation. You can aim to listen, hear and see what the other person is feeling or needing, without judgment. We also have to learn, however, to recognise what we are feeling and needing ourselves, again without judgment. This is achieved by learning and practising a four-step VAK process beginning with an evaluation-free behavioural description of the situation, followed by a statement of one's own feeling and the identification of what your needs are in the situation. From this comes a request of the other person that is practical and feasible:

1. Identifying what I am seeing (V) and hearing (A) without any form of value judgment. (You can practise this by writing purely behavioural descriptions of an incident – I have used incidents in TV soaps to practise this.)

2. Checking for what I am feeling (K), followed by an identification of its source. Use the sentence structure, "I am feeling X because I …" (not "because you …").
   NB: If you start with "I am feeling *that* …" then what comes next is a thought not a feeling!

3. Then clarifying what need is currently driving my behaviour. This can usually be gleaned by backtracking from the anxiety underlying the feeling in Step 2.

4. Finally, what requests can I make of the student in practicable, doable, "now" language and not in the language of demand or threat or of positional power?

As an example, stop and read the following sentence:

"You frighten me speechless when you're really angry."

How would you feel if someone said that to you? What emotions does that switch on inside you? What image comes into your mind? How do you feel towards the speaker?

Now read this next sentence:

"I cannot speak when you raise your voice and wave your arms in the air."

Do you think you can notice the different effect it has on you? How does it alter how you feel towards the speaker this time? How different might your response be?

The first way of communicating contains a judgment about the other person (that he's angry) together with a powerful emotional self-descriptor ("frighten"). Both of these are more likely to deepen the confrontation and lead to conflict, rather than ease it, as they could heighten the listener's own primary anxiety and provoke further distorted responses. The second is a behavioural, sensory-based communication – a judgment-free descriptor of both parties' behaviour – and therefore has less room for misunderstanding and conflict.

This approach containing only self-referenced, nonjudgmental, behavioural descriptions forms the basis of assertive responses to difficult situations. They can be useful exercises in emotional intelligence. The four-step "DESC" approach is one example of an assertive communication script:

1. **D**escribe your feelings, making sure you own them by starting with "I": "I feel disappointed and let down …" (the K)

2. **E**xplain why: "When you do/say X …" (behavioural description – the V and A)

You can pause at this point to gauge the listener's response and decide where to go next depending on whether her reaction is combative, defensive, apologetic, hurt or whatever. When you have handled any response, you can move on and:

3. **S**pecify the future desired behavioural change: "In future, I would prefer it if you would …" (a way of meeting your need)

At this point, depending upon the response you had above, you can stop. The final step, if needed, is to outline clearly the …

4. **C**onsequences, if the unwanted behaviour persists: "Otherwise, I will Z."

The DESC script is often used with the "broken record" technique when the listener leaps in after Step 1 to deny or challenge your feelings. The technique is to repeat the statement of Step 1 word for word. Most listeners will fall silent after three such repeats.

Using counselling approaches

"To jaw-jaw is always better than to war-war."
– Winston Churchill, White House speech, 1954
(quoted in *New York Times*)

Counselling is a three-stage activity: first, it is having the capacity to be a good listener; second, it is having the ability to understand accurately the meaning of what is being said; third, it is the flexibility to respond appropriately. Overall, it means paying close attention to the pupil to create a safe atmosphere that allows them to acknowledge their anxieties, while closing down any internal "interference" from your own anxieties, emotions or self-talk. The three elements can be summarised as:

- Active listening;
- Empathetic understanding;
- *Live* responding.

As a teacher you will have better active listening skills than most. However, it is not easy to give a child your undivided attention in a class of thirty pupils. There are many distractors that get in the way. Some will be external – the noise from the rest of the class, the proximity of another pupil – and some will be internal and therefore less obvious, particularly in a conflict situation. These include:

- *Rehearsing:* forming your answer to an anticipated student reply.
- *Mind-reading:* guessing at some supposed hidden meaning or motivation for the behaviour.
- *Filtering:* selective listening – just hearing the bits that support your mind-reading above.

- *Defending:* addressing your own anxiety about handling the confrontation or your appearance to others.
- *Disagreeing:* sending out the message that the speaker has not been listened to.
- *Comparing:* this relates to the sameness/difference meta-program: "Have I dealt with this sort of problem before? Is this like something that has happened to me before?".
- *Blaming:* prejudging the pupil's culpability in the confrontation and being closed to the chance that you may be wrong in your understanding.
- *Drifting in concentration:* paying attention to other things, ideas or people.

Active listening is composed of a number of micro-skills:

- *Clarifying* – getting the facts without blaming, classifying or labelling; using the metamodel to check/clarify facts, feelings, context, their meaning, and what the student would like to happen next.
- *Paraphrasing* – giving a precise response that captures the essence of the speaker's message (including vocabulary/ phrases he has used in his replies).
- *Challenging* – questioning the validity of what you are hearing; done appropriately, it helps the student reassess his behaviour: "You just said X ... now you seem to be saying Y?" (said questioningly to soften the challenge).
- *Summarising* – accurately reflecting back the big picture – what has been said or what action has been agreed: "So, overall, you ... is that right? Have I got it right?"

It also demands a range of skilled questions and the appropriate use of silence and minimal prompts to keep the student talking. To respond empathically you will have to acknowledge and affirm the student's feelings (expressed or unexpressed) by reflecting them back to the speaker. You can do this both consciously and unconsciously:

- Consciously, through your paraphrasing and summarising: "It seems that you feel ..."
- Unconsciously, through nonverbal rapport, through your body language, voice tone etc.

Solution-focused brief counselling

Because of the constraints within which teachers work, this is a very successful approach to improving the behaviour of pupils. It uses the tenets and processes of "brief therapy", the key principles of which are:

- *Focus on success – use "solution talk".* Communication with the child should have future solutions as their focus and not the past problem as a focus. This entails asking such questions as "What is better now?" Brief counselling avoids problem analysis – a description of what works is better than an explanation of why it failed (*how* to get a solution rather than why you have the problem). Insight into the root cause is not a prerequisite of change, as it can all too easily become a rationalisation for *not* changing.
- *Every problem behaviour has within it the exception, the counterexample of the desired behaviour that can lead to a long-term solution.* Seek the time when the behaviour was absent. Ask the child, "What have you noticed when you behaved this way?" (This is also the basis of the successful NLP strategy for the curing of unwanted allergies.)

(These first two steps are often incorporated into the strategy of asking the child to describe in sensory terms her "miracle day". What would she be doing, seeing, feeling and hearing if, when she awoke tomorrow, all her problems had gone away and everything was going really well. This is a good strategy for getting young children to talk in cases of suspected bullying.)

You can also stimulate "outcome thinking" by asking such questions as:

- "What would you rather have (happen)?"
- "How would you like to feel?"
- "And when you've changed, what differences will you notice? What will you see around you? What will you hear? What will you feel?"

You can strengthen this by asking them to describe these future changes in the present tense, as if they had already happened. "What are you seeing … hearing … feeling?"

- *Small steps can lead to a long journey.* Seize the small improvements as evidence of change. Huge jumps in behaviour demand changes in beliefs and that may need a little more time.

- *All goals are stated positively.* This aligns with the NLP finding that the unconscious mind cannot process a negative consciously. So say what you want in the way you want it to be.

- *Use their language.* There is a branch of counselling that uses "clean" language. This means that, as far as possible, only the language and vocabulary of the client is used. It is uncontaminated by the listener's own speech preferences. It ensures that the conversation remains in the mental map of the child and is therefore going to be more meaningful to them.

- *At some level, children know what's best for them.* This is a belief that the child knows what to do improve behaviour. However, it does not follow that they know how to do it. We often make this mistake with learning itself. (See Blackerby, 1996)

- If what you're doing works – do more of it.

- If what you're doing doesn't work, do something different! (This is another basic presupposition of NLP.)

"Clean" language

This way of carrying on a conversation springs from counselling and is particularly applicable to behavioural problems. It aims to convey three messages to the unconscious mind of the listener:

1. An acknowledgment and affirmation of the pupil's situation and issues;
2. An indirect instruction to begin to think more widely about the issue/ problem;
3. An invitation to explore the student's own thinking to increase their ability to resolve the issue.

The term "clean language" comes from the fact that the teacher attempts to use predominantly the pupil's own words. Earlier in the book, I emphasised the fact that the words we use to describe our experiences are abstractions of the experiences themselves. They are also often metaphoric. What an individual word means to a pupil, therefore, is what meanings and experiences that pupil attaches to it. The meanings two individuals attach to a word are unlikely to be a perfect match, since they spring from different life experiences. There must be a high enough degree of overlap, otherwise all communication between the two people would fail!

The first skill of using a clean-language approach is to refrain from using words of your own and thus avoid "contamination" of the pupil's ideas and meanings. Since it is practically impossible to carry on a conversation without introducing your own words, the second skill is to signal they are yours by marking them out tonally. You can do this by slowing down the tempo of your speech at these words and/or speaking them in a more rhythmic fashion. The process seems stilted and artificial at first, but it is surprising how, after a little practice, the student detects nothing unusual in the conversational manner. The third skill lies in the construction of statements and questions that you frame to help the student move forward by examining their own metaphoric language. The detailed syntax of clean language is beyond the scope of this book, but a clear exposition can be found in Lawley and Tompkins (2000):

T: What do you want?

P: I've hit a brick wall …

T: And what kind of brick wall is that brick wall? (*This is one of a number of standardised ways of replying to reflect back their metaphor.*)

P: A bloomin' big one!

T: And when the brick wall is a blooming big one, is there anything else about that brick wall? (*A second standardised response.*)

P: Yeah, I just can't get past it – it makes me fed up.

T: And you can't get past it and you get fed up. And as you get fed up, what kind of fed up is that? (*A third response from the standardised repertoire.*)

P: It's like nobody ever helps me in this school. You're always helping the bright kids …

As you can see from this snippet, clean language becomes a process that helps children explore their own metaphors (in this case, a brick wall) and their own internal mental map to arrive at a solution to the problem. The skill is to carry on asking the questions in a naturalistic way and avoiding sounding like a computerised robot. This can be done as long as you maintain your respect for and your empathy and rapport with, the speaker.

Key conclusions

- The meta-model of language can be used to change a student's perceptions by filling in the deleted information, smoothing out the "distortions" they have imposed on the experience, and challenging unhelpful generalisations.
- Hypnotic language structures allow the child space to create new perceptions of their experience and extend their choice of appropriate behaviours.
- Greater rapport with pupils and mutual understanding can be gained by speaking to them using metaphors or stories that parallel their experience.
- There is a large range of linguistic techniques that you can learn to use with great effect in managing and motivating children.

Sources and further reading for this chapter

Arbinger Institute, 2000, *Leadership and Self-Deception: Getting Out of the Box*, Berrett-Koestler, San Francisco, CA.

Blackerby, D A, 1996, *Rediscover the Joy of Learning*, Success Skills, Oklahoma City, OK.

De Bono, Edward, 1982, *Lateral Thinking for Management: A Handbook*, Pelican Books, Middlesex, England.

Dilts, R, 2001, *Sleight of Mouth*, Meda Publications, Capitola, CA.

Glasser, W, 1998, *Choice Theory in the Classroom*, Harper Perennial, New York.

Gordon, G, 1996, *Managing Challenging Children*, Prim-Ed Publishing, Greenwood Western Australia.

Haddawy, H (tr.), 1990, *The Arabian Nights*, M. Mahdi (ed.), W W Norton & Co., New York.

Lawley, J, and Tompkins, P, 2000, *Metaphors in Mind: Transformation Through Symbolic Modelling*, Developing Company Press, London.

Lewis, N, 1994, *The Book of Babel: Words and the Way We See Things*, Viking, London.

Pinker, S, 1994, *The Language Instinct: A New Science of Language and Mind*, Penguin, London.

Rogers, W A, 1992, *Managing Teacher Stress*, Pitman, London.

Rosenberg, M B, 1999, *Non-violent Communication: A Language of Compassion*, PuddleDancer Press, Encinitas, CA.

Sklare, G B, 1997, *Brief Counseling that Works: A Solution-Focused Approach for School Counselors*, Corwin Press, Thousand Oaks, CA.

Chapter Five
The Scripts

Speech to calm the anxieties and raise self-esteem

Remember that to increase the likelihood of good learning behaviours rather than dysfunctional ones you will have to create a supportive, anxiety-free environment. The first step is to frame the start of all lessons positively using all the three preferred accessing modes (V, A and K) and the 4-MAT approach of *why? what? how? what if?*, first giving the big picture "what". Then create an agreement frame – i.e., get their unconscious minds to say "yes" to you to start with: "It's Tuesday. You're all sitting down, and today we're going to look at X ..."

When these are all true, they will have mentally agreed with you three times before the lesson proper begins. Then use guided visualisations as a mental rehearsal for doing the task and gaining the learning from it to extend the agreement outlook. Most framing like this starts lessons with embedded commands:

- I'm not sure that *you will find this easier than you think* ... but ...
- Don't think that *you will finish this comfortably by break time*. However ...

These and the following are examples of setting a positive frame around work to help maintain the self-esteem and motivation of the learners:

- This is the same sort of exercise as you did yesterday, but slightly different because it ...

(Since this is a sameness-with-difference statement, it will reassure the majority of the members of the class because it connects what they already know to what they are about to learn.)

- Because it's new, some parts of the exercise will be hard ...

Preframing in this way helps maintain self-esteem in the face of problems as it gives individuals permission to feel confused or stretched by the exercise. Even when a child is completely blocked, one more attempt at the exercise without risking a loss of motivation can be encouraged by a reminder of the potential-difficulty warning:

- Remember, I said at the beginning that some of it would be hard …

Centring scripts

The second possibility is to install a good state for learning through centring. There are different ways of doing this to suit different age groups. You could ask the class, as they sit or stand, to place their feet flat on the floor and to imagine a fishing line hanging from the ceiling, attached to their collars, gently tugging them upwards. Then ask them to plant their feet firmly on the floor and imagine all their weight flowing down into their feet, and ask what that feels like. Tell them to notice their breathing and to imagine breathing from deep in their stomachs, slowly, watching, listening and feeling the movement of their breath in and out of their body. Then ask them to notice that their stomach area is the centre of gravity of their body and that all their energy comes from there. This usually has a sufficiently calming effect for any emotional turmoil to cease. This is because breathing deeply from the diaphragm turns off the sympathetic nervous system, which promotes the fight/flight response, and turns on the more calming parasympathetic nervous system.

Another way is to use the Brain Gym technique "hook-ups". Ask the children to sit upright in the chair, extend their legs and cross them at the ankles, right over left. Then instruct them to stretch out both arms in front of them; twist them so that the backs of their hands face inward to each other. Now, pass the right over the left and cross them at the wrist so that the palms are facing each other and then clasp hands, intertwining their fingers. Then move the clasped hands in a circle by moving downwards and twisting them upwards until they are resting on the chest and the elbows are pointing downwards. The final step is to ask them to touch the top of their palate with the tip of their tongue. They then sit like this for six breaths. After that, they can unclasp hands and ankles and place their feet flat on the floor and their hands on their knees. And sit like this for six more breaths. Carla Hannaford in her book *Smart Moves* says that this is her most used Brain Gym exercise and describes how she uses it with children who have been disruptive, to help them calm down and prepare to discuss their behaviour.

Alternatively, you could ask them to think about all the parts that make up their whole self:

> Think about your thoughts ... your thoughts are part of you, but they are not all of you ... consider your feelings, you have feelings ... sense how you're feeling now ... but your feelings are not the total you ... you have a body ... and even your body is not all of you ... you have ideas in your mind that go beyond your body ... you have all these different parts to you and sometimes ... you can be aware that they are all coming together now ... in one place inside your body, centred somewhere just below your stomach ... below your navel ... when you can feel complete and relaxed and alert ... ready to begin ...

For young children I have found a physical balancing approach useful. As in the first example, get them to stand with their feet pointing forward and about shoulder width apart. Using the fishing-line visualisation, encourage them to lengthen and straighten their spine. And then to rock gently forwards and then backwards, making the rocking movements smaller and smaller until they find the position where they are in balance – leaning neither forwards nor backwards, but perfectly upright. Then they slowly rock from side to side. Once again, the rocking is to get smaller and smaller until they are in the middle position – leaning neither to the left nor to the right. Then they just slightly bend their legs and imagine that their thoughts are down in their stomach. By this time most pupils are calmer and more collected and ready for learning.

Such exercises can be strengthened by the use of a "trancing" script such as the following, for anxiety management. This should be spoken quietly but quite rapidly:

As you sit there, close your eyes and then just lift your eyes up to the sky under your eyelids, almost until it hurts, and then let them fall back to the middle of your head. Then think about the muscles around your eyes and begin to relax them. Imagine you can relax them so much that your eyelids just will not work. Pretend that your eyelids just will not work … they just won't work …

And then let that relaxed feeling go all down through your body down to your toes … that's right [*as you watch for signs of their relaxing*] … Now place the palm of your right hand just below your bellybutton … and then … quietly rest … your left had over your right … that's right … Now relax there awhile in the quiet and then watch for those thoughts and feelings that come into your mind … just look and listen for the pictures or sounds that come into your mind … . That's good! … Pictures, thoughts words or noises or feelings – whatever comes in – and just watch and listen … just observe them all, and, as you find yourself wandering, just return to watching and listening … [longer pause]

… good …

Now imagine yourself in the future, when you find yourself angry [or sad, or afraid, or anxious] … just place your hands on your stomach again and go inside and watch and listen to what's going on there … inside … and keep breathing … slowly … and notice how the [anger/sadness/fear] goes away … until it has completely gone …

So … leaving behind everything that you need to leave, let yourself become alert [or wide awake] again and return in your own way, bringing with you all that new understanding. And I want you to know you can do this any time you wish.

Another calming script is adapted from one that is often used in yoga classes:

Make yourself comfortable in your seat. You are going to notice your breathing … as you become more comfortable you can begin to pay attention to you breath … how it comes in … and how it goes out again … in … and … out. And as you notice your breath, begin counting your breath each time you breathe in … counting to ten, then begin again with one. When your mind wanders – and all our minds wander – gently bring it back to "one" and start counting again. Notice when your mind wanders so you can learn to recognise it happening … you can have more self-control over where it goes to … and so when you are ready to … come back into this room and be comfortable and truly ready for today's lesson.

Addressing the specific anxieties

For individual children, their self-esteem can be maintained more effectively by targeting feedback at the child's primary anxiety and specific needs, where you can identify them. It is even more powerful when used with the appropriate learning-style language.

Performance anxiety – decreasing "fight"

Pupils coming out of this anxiety often misbehave if they perceive that the tasks they are given are not very challenging or demanding, that they are unnecessarily restricted in their choice of task, or that the task is a waste of time. Remember that the associated behaviour is fight – aggressive resistance to the task. Language that gets the best out of them includes words and phrases to do with challenge, choice, the chance to compete, potential rewards and the element of risk. On completion of their tasks, they want to be noticed, commended and appreciated for getting it done. Remind them of past successes to reinforce their concept of being in control of their progress:

- This will be a stretch for you.
- I wonder if … you can really do this.
- Let's see if you can finish this first.
- Which of these two exercises would you want to do first? The choice is yours.
- If you can find the answer to this then, you can choose to …
- Don't … do this today … unless … you really think you can do this
- I like the way you …
  - get on with your work.
  - are always prepared to get stuck in straight away.
  - finish on time.
  - get things done.
  - are creative at finding a way through the problem.

- are persuasive at getting the group working.
- responded to John; you managed that well.

Acceptance anxiety – decreasing "freeze"

Children with this anxiety uppermost in their minds are demotivated if they perceive themselves to be ignored, treated unfairly or insensitively, or harshly judged. They are more likely to misbehave if treated sarcastically or aggressively and misbehaviour here is centred on submission – they will not openly resist, but delay or subvert the task. Motivating them calls for them to be talked to (and listened to), accepted and appreciated. Compliments that they will respond best to include such descriptors as "friendly", "considerate", "supportive", "sincere", "unselfish" and "modest". They often don't need to be forever the centre of attention, but they do need consistent, regular appreciation. They want to know that you recognise their special talents:

- You really get on well with most people in this class, don't you?
- I like the way you're behaving now: I noticed you helping Anne with her work when I was busy just now – thank you. I value that in this class.
- So … if I understand you correctly, you …
- I like …
    - the way you're helpful to everyone else in your group.
    - how considerate and thoughtful you are.
    - how you just quietly help the others without making a song and dance about it.
    - how modest you are about the part you've played.
    - how you were much more cooperative with your group today.

Orientation anxiety –decreasing "flight"

These children tend to work cautiously, carefully and methodically. They do not like to be hurried, and faced with what they perceive to be too much pressure to finish, may descend into helplessness and inactivity. Motivating language for them has to reassure them that they will have the time to be thorough and to think things through for themselves. It will also have to contain clear step-by-step instructions. In terms of McCarthy's 4-MAT, they are often the children who start in the "Why" quadrant – they need to have a satisfactory reason for doing the task. A good "reason" in schoolwork is often one linked to their previous work. Older children may not like an overfriendly teaching approach, preferring a "proper" distance between themselves and you. Compliments will contain appreciation of the care they take, the precision of their work and how they work methodically, taking everything into consideration. They also need to know that you are "fair" in your dealings with them and others:

- There should be enough time for you to do all this exercise carefully.
- I can just let you get on and do this, because I know you'll work accurately.
- This builds on last week's exercise and will enable you to …
- Each step is written on the handout …
- I can see you're making real progress …
- I like …
  - how carefully you do everything.
  - how thorough all your work is.
  - how you always think things through first before rushing in.
  - how you always do your bit in the group.

Remember: Prevention is better than cure and the best way to pre-empt the occurrence of the first three Fs (see Table 3.8) is to ensure that your teaching is scattered with the fourth F – fun – even if you have to incorporate spontaneous outbreaks of fun in your lesson planning! In addition to the use of these specific vocabularies, you can use constructive reframing as described in Chapter Three. Remember, the process is:

1. *State any negative statements positively (NLP's first criterion for good goals is to say what you want, not what you don't want).*
"I don't want John talking to me when I'm working."
Surface reframe: "You want John to stop disturbing you."
Deeper reframe: "You need quiet to work well."

2. *Use nonviolent communication approaches to neutralise blame and accusations and yet preserve the underlying issue:*
"Mike always swears at me."
"You don't like the way Mike speaks to you."

3. *Change (rather than ignore or avoid) any derogatory remarks.*
"Dave must be thick because I warned him I'd hit him if he didn't stop calling me names."
"You want Dave to leave you in peace and are frustrated that things haven't changed."

4. *Acknowledge and affirm any feelings you hear expressed – this is the return message that reassures the child that they are being heard.*
"Jane's been saying stupid things about me."
"You feel hurt about what's been said." (This said enquiringly, since it is an assumption on your part and may not be true for the speaker.)

Using the meta-program patterns

Imagine a pupil having difficulty with graphs, whose motivation strategies are based on the meta-programs:

1. Prefers options to procedures;
2. Works from the big picture or handles information in large chunks;
3. Looks for differences rather than sameness;
4. Has a move-away-from stance rather than a towards-goals one.

A totally mismatched approach would be for the teacher to:

1. Stress the "correct" way to do these problems;
2. Give very specific details on which problems to do, in which order, and how to do them;
3. Emphasise that they were basically the same sort of problems that were done last lesson;
4. Emphasise, too, that the target was to finish them all so that everyone could get out at playtime on time.

For this "pupil", an approach such as this would be guaranteed to turn them off! Matching the student better would be an approach that said something like:

These problems are a different kettle of fish to yesterday's [meta-program 3], though you could solve them using the same sort of approach. However, I'll be happy if you find another way of doing them [meta-

> program 1] so long as you can do them all [meta-program 2] in this lesson, so you won't have to work into your break time [meta-program 4].

On the other hand, a different pupil with the same problem and the same meta-programs – but with the opposite polarities – is likely to respond better to an approach that follows the four steps outlined above:

> These problems are very similar to yesterday's [meta-program 3] and so you could solve them using almost the same approach especially, if I show you the extra steps [meta-program 1], one at a time [meta-program 2], you will have to take, so that you can finish them on time [meta-program 4].

Some of the more powerful words and phrases that you can direct at each pupil with the particular meta-program to motivate them better are contained in Table 5.1.

Using the meta-model

Remember, the meta-model is used to improve your understanding of the child's mental map: to get below the superficial communication and uncover the child's own understanding of the world and the meanings they attach to events (see Table 5.2).

Gestalt approaches

Much of the meta-model had its basis in the work of the Gestalt therapist Fritz Perls. This approach was aimed at helping people become more aware of how they interact with other people. You can use it with children to help them understand their interaction with the others in the classroom, so that they can choose to experiment with new ways of behaving. A key idea of Gestalt therapy is that individuals will grow and develop by becoming more aware of what they are, rather than in trying to be different. For example, "If I want to improve my decision making I will learn more by understanding how I make them now, rather than by trying to make decisions differently."

Table 5.1: Motivating language for the "mental" meta-programs

1. Processing

Large chunks	*Small chunks*
Overall; the main thing to understand; just get this one thing; what really counts is; end of the day; just remember	specifically; each step will; the first detail; first this and then that; after that; the order will be

2. Matching

Sameness	*Difference*
This is the same as; similar to; just like before; identical to; you already know; in common with; you've seen this before	This is new, strange, unique; unlike anything you've done so far; the first time; the first and only time you will be able to

3. Proactive

Proactive	*Reactive*
Let's get started; get it done right away; off you go; what are you waiting for?; let's hurry; be brave; get stuck in	think about it first; really understand what's involved; get the first step right; are you clear about each stage?

4. Motivational direction

Towards	*Away from*
You'll get; achieve; attain; then you can; here's what you'd gain; you'll be able to; the benefit will be	Then you will stop; prevent; not need to; you won't have to; the problem will then disappear

5. Focus of attention

Internal	*External*
It's up to you; decide what you think; can you feel OK about that?; you might consider; you're in the best position to decide	Your mother will like it; I think that; everybody likes that sort of thing; the other group has done it really well this way; everyone will notice that

6. Working style

Alone	*Near to*	*Collectively*
It's down to you; by yourself; your responsibility; all your own work	You'll do this; they will do that; you can talk, but do your own working out	Together; share, you'll all need to take a part; this team

7. Convincer pattern

Visual (see)	*Auditory (hear)*	*Kinaesthetic (do)*
Can I show you?; do you see?; is it clearer?; get the picture?; how do you view that?	Does that sound right to you?; ring bells?; are you in tune with that?; what does that tell you?; say to you?	Have you grasped it?; does that feel OK; try it out; does that make sense now?; have you made the connection?

8. Options

Options	*Procedures*
Here's your chance to; opportunity to; here are the options; it's up to you; it's your choice; try a different way	First, and then; this is the right way; this is the tried-and-tested method; just follow the instructions

Table 5.2: Precision questions – the meta-model in use

Language pattern	Clarification strategy
Deletions	
Simple deletions	*Recover the missing information*
I am angry.	About what? About whom?
They don't care about me.	Who, specifically, doesn't care?
She's a better teacher.	Better than whom? Better at what, compared with what?
Unspecified verbs	*Recover the behaviour*
He annoys me.	How, specifically, does he annoy you?
Lack of referential index	*Recover the subject*
Everyone hates me.	Who, specifically?
Nominalisations	*Change the noun back into a verb*
Communication is bad here.	Who's not communicating what to whom?
Generalisations	
Universals	*Challenge the generalisation*
I always miss out.	Always?
I could never do that.	Never? What would happen if you did?
Possibilities	*Challenge the impossibility*
I can't possibly do that.	What stops you? What would happen if you did?
Necessities	*Challenge the necessity*
I have to do that.	What would happen if you didn't?
Distortions	
Mind reading	*Find the fantasy*
She doesn't like me because :	How do you know? How does it mean she doesn't like you?
Lost performative	*Find the actor*
It's not right to …	Who says it's not right? According to whom? How do you know it's not right?
Poor cause–effect links	*Find the actions*
She makes me angry.	How specifically? How does what she does cause you to become angry?
False equivalences	*Challenge the link*
She's a poor teacher, she's always telling me off.	How does her telling you off mean she's a poor teacher?
Presuppositions	*Uncover unspoken assumptions*
If you knew how difficult it is, you wouldn't do that.	How do you know I don't know? What am I doing exactly?

Self-acceptance is the initial step to beginning the development of emotional intelligence. The second step is your own use of language and, through it, an appreciation of where you place the responsibility for your actions and what is happening to you. So a first step for you into this is perhaps to encourage children to recast the way they describe events, to repeat what they say but with a change in a key word. Some of the most powerful words to bring about changes in children's mindscapes and therefore their behaviour are given below. For example, "In school, I *have* to … or else …" is replaced by "At school, I *choose* to … because …"

Changing our language in this way changes our focus, from being externally referenced to meet other people's expectations, to being internally referenced to take ownership of our own behaviour. Examples of unproductive speech habits and how they could be rephrased are shown in Table 5.3.

Using the Milton model and other "hypnotic" scripts and strategies

Milton Erickson used language patterns that pushed the listener into going inside his own thoughts, through deliberately distorting, deleting and generalising what he said to them. Remember, deliberately vague language is designed to allow the listener to make his own sense of the words he is hearing. That way he agrees with everything that is said, because it's *his* sense. Erickson would frame sentences so as to improve rapport with his clients and to lead them into a relaxed state so that they could explore their issues in their mind, redefine the problem and arrive at a possible solution. Examples of such questions are given in Table 5.4.

Table 5.3: Gestalt language shifts

These changes in speech patterns form part of the much more comprehensive structure of the meta-model. One of the best ways to become familiar with these vocabulary shifts is to learn to apply them to yourself. You can listen to your own speech and notice which of the words and phrases you use most frequently. When you notice them, begin to restate them as directed by the table. Notice how different you feel when you say them and also the differences in the way others respond to you. You can achieve even bigger shifts by listening to your "internal" speech – those things you say to yourself when in anxious or emotional situations. Notice how often you say such things as "I can't, I should, I ought, I must" when talking about your own behaviour or capabilities. Or how often you state things in the passive voice when describing situations in which you didn't do something.

Changing

"It" to **"I"**
It's a waste of time. / I think I'm wasting my time.
It's a pain being in this class. / I don't like being in this class.

"You" to **"I"**
You'll enjoy going to see … / I enjoyed going to see …
You're not appreciated here. / I'm not appreciated here.

"We" to **"I"**
We ought to think about it. / I want to think about it.
We should slow down and be more careful. / I'm concerned about making mistakes. / I want to go more slowly.

"can't" to **"won't"**
I just can't stop it. / I just won't stop it.
I can't face her. / I won't face her.

"need" and **"must"** to **"want"**
I must do this now. / I want to do this now.
I must do well. / I want to do well.
I need your help. / I want your help.

"have to" to **"choose to"**
I have to be there early. / I choose to be there early.

"know" to **"imagine"**
I just know it will go wrong. / I just imagine it will go wrong.
I know she'll be angry. / I imagine she'll be angry.

"but" to **"and"**
I agree, but don't you think … / I agree, and I think …
I want to, but they won't let me. / I want to and I imagine they will try to stop me.
I'd like to but I can't right now. / I'd like to and yet I won't right now.

passive statements into **active ones**
The work didn't get done. / I didn't do the work.
There was no chance to speak. / I didn't take the opportunity to air my view.

Table 5.4: Milton model statements

Language filter	Milton model statements – the meta-model patterns in reverse
Deletions	**Simple deletions** Statements that need an object to make complete sense *You are feeling uncomfortable* _____ **Unspecified verbs** Verbs that obscure the actual behaviour or sensory experience *And you can begin to change your behaviour, now* **Nominalisations** Verbs converted into nouns, actions treated as things *Your* friendships *in this class depend totally on your own* behaviour **Lack of referential index** Statements that need a specific subject to make complete sense *Stay calm! It'll all come out in the wash*
Generalisation	**Universals** Words that assume that a single event can be extended to all situations, or all times, to all people etc *Every time you begin to feel angry, you can remember one of the ways to alter that feeling, can't you?* **Possibilities** Statements that define the speaker's limits of their capabilities, choices and actions because of what they believe is possible *Honestly, algebra is something you can learn now or in a short while.* **Necessities** Statements that assume an unwritten law, for the speaker and/or for everyone *One thing you know is that you must feel OK to carry on learning this*
Distortions	**Mind-reading** Stating things that are imagined as real *I know that you are the sort of learner who will stick at this and see it through* **Lost performatives** Value statements that omit who is doing the valuing or who is being judged *This is good because it will make all the difference to how you get on* **Poor cause–effect links** Assumption that statement A leads directly to statement B with no proof *Getting to grips with this section now will make a lot of other maths problems easier to solve in the future*

False equivalences
Assumption that statement A is the same as a different
statement, B
>   *You are doing good work now, so you must be pleased with your
>   maths*

Presuppositions
Unspoken assumptions behind the words, taken as true
>   *I wonder how quickly you will learn this vocabulary*

Example of a Milton vague communication

So, as you begin to read this, I guess (and it's a good thing to make such guesses, now … and again) … because it means … you are learning everything you need from this book as all those things … everything, that you can learn … give you new insights. And you can, can't you? – learn, that is, by reading. And it's more or less the right thing for you right now, isn't it? I mean, while you are holding this book here, reading these words consciously, it means your unconscious mind is also here and can hear these words. And, since that is true, it's not right for me to tell it – learn these patterns now, or later – let it learn them any way it wishes, in any order. Do you feel this … is it something you can understand? Because Richard Bandler says that books like this talk to your unconscious mind more than your conscious mind. Whether you begin to use the scripts in this book straightaway or later is not so important because I know you are a reflective teacher – and it's good to be a reflective teacher, as reflective teachers are successful. And successful classroom management is every teacher's goal, isn't it?

Embedded commands

The above example, if heard live, would have had sent some embedded commands to your unconscious mind. The following are examples of multilevel communication for behaviour management that you can use in the classroom. Remember that for the unconscious mind to hear the subliminal instruction contained in the sentence, it has to be marked out in some way. There are several ways in which to accomplish this. It might be just an 'umm':
"Why don't you … umm face me now … while you …"

Or, better, it could be a slight change in tone: a lower pitch, a change in speed, a slightly slower rate of speaking. It could be bracketed by a barely noticeable pause either side of the command – a slightly longer-than-normal gap between your words. Or it could be signalled visually by a gesture: a waving hand, a pointed finger, nods of the head, a lifting of an eyebrow. Practise and find out which work best for you and your pupils.

After working so hard yesterday, you will ... *find today's writing easier* ... which means ...

I'm wondering if ... *you can agree with me that* ...

I don't suppose you can ... *imagine being able to do this easily* ...

I'm not saying you will ... *do this exercise quickly* ... however, you will ... *find it easier* ... than you think

Can't you ... *see yourself doing it*, can't you?

Why don't you ... *face me now* ... while you ...

I'm not suggesting that ... *you will finish it all by break time* ... and yet when you ...

And when you go home I want you to tell someone about how ... *you have done well today*

I wouldn't want you to ... *just forget your anger for now* ... because what I ...

Regardless of how difficult it might look, I'm asking how ... *you could do it all*

I'm not sure if ... *you can think of a different way of doing this*, ... *can't you?* [The "can't you?" is another strengthener]

Please put your book on my desk, as you go over to ... *tidy up your table*

Couldn't you ... *imagine yourself doing it* ...

Don't ... *forget that it might be difficult* ... and then ... *have another go*

It's not likely that just by listening to me, you won't … *change the way you behave right now* … won't you?

You may not … *have a clear idea now* … of what you want to happen

I'm sure you couldn't … *imagine, could you, that the problem will just disappear* … when you …?

I'm not going to say … *this is easy to learn* … however …

I suppose you can't … *imagine being able to solve this* … just now, but …

I am not sure … *you can learn to do this easily* … yet … when …

I suspect … *they will be easier to do* … than you think

Regardless of how difficult it seems just now, I'm asking you how … *you could do it simply* …

I'm not going to suggest to you that … *you will be totally comfortable working on this* … except when you …

I'll be with you in a minute, but I expect … *you can work it out yourself* …

This commanding of the unconscious mind points up the potential poisoning of a young mind and the erosion of self-esteem of such comments as "Don't be silly", "Don't be so thick".

An example of a guided visualisation

Any script is merely indicative of an approach. You will tailor your scripts in both content and language to suit its purpose and your audience. A key principle is to allow pupils the right to opt out of the activity. Other important factors are those of space and comfort, so that pupils can be seated comfortably, with arms folded, or with head on arms on the table or desk. The risks of interruption and outside noise must be minimised. Appropriate background music can be very helpful in creating the right environment. You can make a tape recording of your trial scripts to experiment with, before trying them out in class.

A guided visualisation is useful in preparing a group for a lesson. A description of the process couched in such phraseology as "imagine that you …" followed by a straightforward description can be very effective. Any mental rehearsal of a process utilises the same neural pathways in the brain as when you actually do it. A more "hypnotic" script might run as follows:

> Just close your eyelids and let your mind go where it wants. And you may soon … *become aware of your breathing* … whether it is fast or slow, deep or shallow. And just let yourself *be aware of your breathing*, in and out, while, as … you are hearing me speak … you are conscious of my voice and your unconscious … mind is also awake and listening. You know, don't you, that we all have FIVE senses through which … *you can learn new things* … but beFORE we start, you can think of the THREE main senses that we mostly use everyday TO learn in school and which everyONE knows about …

> And I wonder when you will realise today … that you are learning at a whole deeper level … of understanding … And it will be easy to … understand graphs [*or any other desired outcome of the lesson*] … because you really want to get a good result today.

> And it's interesting … remembering what you need to remember, and forgetting what you need to forget … It does not matter if you forget, you need not remember what you can forget. Your unconscious … mind remembers everything that you need to know

> So when everyONE honestly begins TO really learn, all of the THREE most important senses have been used FOR taking the information and we've done all that in just FIVE minutes.

Sleight-of-mouth patterns

These patterns describe a range of tactical responses to statements that are based on a belief. They are designed to change that belief. It is a recognition that the focus for change very often is not the event or the current situation, but the *meaning* the pupil attaches to it. So the following are lines of attack on the meanings behind the words used. Taken together, they are a comprehensive kitbag of tools to use in response to an unwanted behaviour consequent on a belief.

For example, the different possible replies to the belief statement "I'm thick – I just can't do graphs" could be:

Challenge the belief
- Listen to you! How true do you think what you've just said really is?
- Is believing it going to be helpful to you in the summer exams?
- You're only saying that at the moment because you haven't yet got the overall picture.

Find a counterexample to the belief
- You did yesterday's bar charts well.
- Do you remember another time when you felt this way? ... like learning to tie your shoes laces? ... And now you know you can do it easily [with Milton language].

This counters the tendency to focus on the problems and forget the successes.

Apply the belief to the believer
- What's stupid is that you should think you are stupid!

Turning the belief back on itself encourages a re-evaluation of the belief.

Apply the belief and behaviour to the listener
- That's hard for me to believe, so will I be stupid if I can't help you?

This helps to highlight incongruities in the pupil's statement.

Test the reality strategy behind the belief
- Where did you learn that finding something hard means that you're stupid?
- When did you decide that finding something hard means that you're stupid?

How do they know this statement is true? How do they think about it?

Put the statement into reverse
- How does finding graphs hard cause you to be stupid?

This forces them to think about whether the reverse statement has any meaning, and subsequently the meaningfulness of the original.

Change the scale of their problem and alter their perspective by ...
1. Generalising upwards
- So far, you are doing well in maths over all, so you will understand this particular section soon, too.

This puts the problems with graphs into their wider success at maths generally.

2. Chunking down to more detail
- Which one graph are you finding difficult, right now?

This stops them "catastrophising" – escalating or generalising the specific problem into a global one: "I can't do this graph so I can't do graphs – full stop."

3. Changing the time frame
- By the end of term you'll wonder what all the fuss was about.

In maths, as in life – all things pass away or move on!

4. Using different criteria or a different model of the world
- Well, for you, a person finding something hard may mean they're stupid, but where I come from it's a good sign because it means the person's giving it their best shot.

This helps them re-evaluate the belief by giving an alternative viewpoint and encourages the question, "Is this true for everyone?"

Redefining one of the words to shift the meaning directly
- You're confused right now about doing graphs.

This changes stupidity to mean something more acceptable: confusion.

Put the focus on the intention behind the statement
- I know your intent is to do well in the test so does this mean you want extra help with these?
- Is this your way of saying you're confused and want more help?
- Is this your way of saying you want to do something else?

This forces them to ask themselves why they are saying this. What is the positive intention of saying it? What do they gain by saying it?

Put the attention on the consequences of the statement
- So if you continue to think you're stupid what does it mean for your work in this class for the rest of the year?
- So if you stick with thinking graphs are too hard, what will happen in the test?

This forces them to think about what will happen if they continue to think this way.

Change outcome
- It's not about whether you think you are stupid or about these graphs: it's really about what you want to do when you go to the sixth form.

This challenges the relevancy to this current belief statement and switches to another issue altogether.

Find an appropriate metaphor
- I think that graphs to you may be like football to a Martian seeing its first match, trying to make out what the rules are ...

This is designed to help them be more open to new possibilities by gaining insights as they stretch the analogy into different aspects.

Change logical level
- You are not stupid [an identity-level statement]: you're just a normal student working hard to understand the way to solve graph problems easily [a behavioural statement] and soon you will have cracked it [a new capability].

You have taken the student from *identity* down two levels to *behaviour*, to go back up one level to *capability*.

A powerful way to use these approaches is to construct a chain of different meanings to get to a positive perspective:

1. When you say you're feeling stupid about graphs, it tells me that you are working hard to understand them [meaning shift No. 1] and ...
2. ... when you are working hard, that means you are approaching these problems intelligently, doesn't it? [meaning shift No. 2] ...
3. ... and you can know that, when you tackle problems thoughtfully, you will find a way through to an answer [meaning shift No. 3] ...
4. ... so saying you're feeling stupid isn't such a bad thing because it tells me that you are working intelligently and will find a solution [final meaning].

The chain has incrementally made 'stupid' into equivalent to 'working intelligently' in this context. The four steps make opposition to the changed meaning less likely than in a direct redefinition.

A miscellany of useful words

Use the following words:

Try – to presuppose failure when you want them *not* to succeed at something.

- I want you to *really* try to find the difficulty here.
  This is strengthened when you deliberately add mismatching language:

- Really *try*, I want you to really *see* [where this is the least used modality – for someone who is primarily an auditory or kinaesthetic learner] if you can ...

Don't – I drew your attention to the use of "don't" in the section on embedded commands. Remember, the unconscious mind will not process the "don't" and will tend to follow the instruction after it. That's why I advocated that you always state what behaviour you want and not what you don't want. "Walk!" rather than "Don't run!" However, you can turn this tendency to your advantage by the careful use of "don't". "Don't for a moment imagine this is easy."

But – however, beware of this word. It doesn't just prepare the listener for a disagreement: it gives them thinking time to start the next round of real conflict. This is because at the deeper level, the mind translates "but" as a denial of everything said prior to it. "I hear you, but ..." sends the message to the unconscious mind that you have most certainly *not* heard. Therefore you can use it to your own advantage as a weakening and negating conjunction.

- You may have thought it difficult but once we finish talking ... *you will find it easier.*

Unless as a strengthener, combined with a negation.

- Don't ... do it the way I showed you ... unless you really want to ... get them finished before you leave.

(This is particularly strong when the first half of the sentence is what you want to happen and the second half is what the child desires as an outcome.)

Stop, followed by an embedded command, as a way of closing down the current thinking to create an opening for something new.

- *Stop* and ... *picture what it could be like* to ...
- *Stop* and ... imagine ... you can do it easily ...

Or where you need to be less authoritative.

- If you were to stop and ... say to yourself ...
- Just for a moment ... *stop* ... and do you ... *believe you can do this* ...

Pretend – an alternative way of tackling a "can't" response.

- Just for a moment, pretend … you can … What would that be like? How would you feel then? What would happen then, once … you can do it?"

Yet – a presuppositional way of regarding a block to learning.

- *I know you can't do it … yet …*

The "yet" sends out the expectation that it is within the pupil's capability and that it is only a matter of time until the block is overcome or got around. It underlines that schooling is about learning and that learning is an evolving process in time, not a one-off and forever event!

Part IV

What Can I Do With This Learning?

Chapter Six
Putting It All Together

Language to improve behaviour – neuro-linguistics in action in your classroom

Watching the tree to catch a hare

Many years ago in China, a naïve young boy was ordered by his master to go out and catch a hare for dinner. Not knowing just how to do this he wandered aimlessly around in the local wood. Suddenly he disturbed a hare, which, leaping from the under-growth, shot at speed across his path, casting him a backward glance, only to run at full pelt into a tree and stun itself. The boy picked up the unconscious hare and returned to his master, proud of his success and pleased with the praise heaped upon him.

The next time he was ordered out to catch a hare he went straight to the tree where he had caught his first hare. He then sat and waited for a hare to appear and stun itself.

And waited … and went home empty-handed.

And the third time he was asked to catch a hare, he went back to the tree and sat and waited.

And the fourth time.

And so on … despite never again catching a hare.

The above passage was first written down 2,000 years ago and is retold by Adeline Yen Mah in her book *Watching the Tree*.

This book may be to you like a travel book of a foreign country, complete with maps and key features of interest. Once you have read it, you should be able to imagine what the country is like: the different landscapes in the different territories; the places that might satisfy your own personal curiosity about the people and their culture. However, without walking on the terrain, without exploring the actual countryside, without talking to the people, the guide remains a book. So explore the country and find new vistas.

It is easy for a teacher, having developed successful teaching strategies and techniques over many years, to continue to rely too much on what worked once, in the face of changing circumstances. We often maintain our long-held beliefs and behaviours in the face of contradictory evidence of the truth of the belief, or the usefulness of the behaviour. Cherishing our personal myths is just being human! The ideas and techniques in this book may be new to you and therefore deploying them may seem risky. But remember: if you want different results, you have to do something different from what you currently do. Once you have decided to improve the behaviour in your classroom by learning these techniques, keep that decision in mind as you use them in your daily exchanges with your pupils. The key factor is belief.

At the beginning of this book I listed some of the main NLP principles, all of which are useful beliefs to hold in relating to other people. Add to those your own belief in yourself and your ability to experiment with different approaches, and then using these language patterns is an easily learned skill.

So, as you come to the end of this book, and think about how you will begin to apply these linguistic patterns, you will, like all good communicators, naturally, put it all together. Remember, everything you have learned counts in communicating effectively and effortlessly! The more you practise some of these language patterns, the more you'll be able to use them unconsciously at the right time. As you continue to learn more of them, you'll find that they become easier to use; and the more you use them, the more you'll understand them – at a subconscious level – and I believe you will become even more effective.

I am not talking only about your language skills: I am talking about raising your effectiveness in classroom management over all. In *Helping the Client*, John Heron said:

> [J]ust as artificial exercises in a gym build up muscle for real physical work, so artificial behavioural exercises in a workshop build up psychological "muscle" for real-life encounters with other people.

Heron recommends that in human relational training we model sports training. Build up specific muscle groups by targeted exercises, and, before any training session, perform stretching exercises. So practice sessions in psychological skills should be preceded by warming-up and stretching exercises. Warm up and stretch your brain's linguistic "muscles". The first thing you can do is a private, internal performance: think about the techniques for getting into a good emotional state yourself using the tracking exercise on page 100 (Chapter Three), or centring (Chapter Five).

Or you could identify your own internal language and use the precision questions of Table 5.2 to confront that dialogue – and change it.

You could choose one of the NLP beliefs about behaviour that you find most difficult to accept. Spend a week "trying it on". Act *as if* you did believe it and notice what differences result. Then revisit your old belief.

Then, when you want to go public, choose a class with which you already have a generally good relationship, so as to be able to practise the skills in a relatively "safe" environment. In acquiring and using new skills, success in the first step is vital. So ensure that you optimise your success as you begin to experiment with the language models.

Second, plan to use just one strategy at a time and wait for what you judge is an appropriate situation for an intervention of this sort. Then notice the level of effectiveness of the intervention and the differences in outcomes between what you achieved and what you might have expected to achieve, given your previous history of such encounters. Only when you can feel comfortable with this new skill, experiment with others and in other classes. The ideas and theories presented here are the results of practical experimentation with people in a wide range of contexts. They are now offered as ideas to be tested in the classroom. Only you can explore their application and decide on their benefits to your personal and professional life. So please experiment. There are many small experiments you can run to develop your skills.

Experiment 1

You could start with the preferred predicates. Choose one or more children (or colleagues) and listen carefully over time to the words they use and identify any leaning towards visual, auditory or kinaesthetic language. Once you have identified them, you could choose someone with a different preferred modality from your own and experiment with your own ability to match that person's language patterns. Then you could spend some time deliberately mismatching and notice the difference in your relationship.

Experiment 2

You could do the same sort of experiment by identifying the meta-programs of chosen pupils or colleagues. As before, when you have identified one or two key ones, start adjusting your own language to match theirs and improve rapport and their motivation. You can use questions such as:

- "Just imagine you are going to change subject/school today. Why would you do that today?" (Meta-program 4 – away from/towards.) Listen to what comes after the "because ..." It will give you the direction – *away* from something in this subject/school or *towards* something desirable elsewhere.

- "How do you know when you've done well in a lesson?" (Meta-program 5 – internal/external.) Do they answer with an affirmation of feeling (internal) or do they seek external proof or approbation?

Experiment 3

Take the opportunity when talking to one or more children in your class to observe their eye movements. Start with those children who quite naturally make large movements, so as to make it easy on yourself. You could have a small number of stock questions that are deliberately couched to prompt visual recall, visual imagination, self-talk and so forth. You can check whether these ideas hold in your own class; whether any left-handed children are 'reversed-wired' in this area; whether you can improve your observation skills to catch smaller and smaller movements.

Experiment 4
When you are comfortable using the above skill, use it to help elicit the decision-making strategy of a colleague or a pupil. You can start with the prompt, "How do you do that?" or "How do you know when to ...?" Watch the eyes and hear the words. You can probe deeper with questions such as "And then what happens?" or "What happens after that?" and "What happens that tells you you've decided?" (This is quite a sophisticated skill and I recommend you read about it in a more comprehensive book on NLP.)

Experiment 5
Bring to mind a child whom you may have described to yourself or a colleague, using judgments or nominalisations: "He's a difficult pupil ..."; "She's so moody ..."; "He's an attention seeker..." Then consider one or more of the events that prompted you to use that label. Write down the actual behaviours using sensory descriptions only. That is, what did you observe?

Being able to construct observational descriptions free of judgments or evaluations is a key skill in giving feedback that can be heard. It is the basis of Marshall Rosenberg's nonviolent communication and, according to him, for the Indian philosopher, Krishnamurti, it is the highest form of intelligence.

Experiment 6
Catch yourself using one of your typical drivers or "modal operators of necessity" (MON): "I really must do X before Y"; "I should go to the meetings ..."; "I always have to be on time ..." Many of these indicate we have set ourselves unrealistically high standards: "I must be a perfect teacher, while being a perfect mother – and a perfect wife"! If you can identify such a standard, rewrite it as a more realistic one – one that you are likely to have some success in attaining. Then write yourself an alternative internal dialogue to replay whenever you catch yourself falling into the trap saying the original statement (or whatever works best for you):

- **MON:** "When I am teaching science I must always know what I am talking about."

- **Realistic standard:** Even the best of scientists "have a robust sense of their own ignorance" (the American physicist and Nobel laureate, Richard Feynman).
- **New internal dialogue:** "It's OK to not know everything in science: by definition, science is the art of enquiring into the unknown. Now and again, I can be an enquirer with the students."

What would it be like if you truly believed your chosen statement? Even if you don't, you can act as if you did. Adopt a physical posture that goes with the statement as if you truly believed it and say it again to yourself. Notice how different it feels.

You can repeat this sort of exercise with other pieces of the meta-model – false equivalences, for example:

- If I get things wrong in science, the pupils will think I am a poor teacher.
- Realistic standard: to err is human.
- New internal dialogue: "My worth as a teacher does not depend on my subject knowledge of science."

Or you could do the exercise using cause–effect links. In fact, you can do similar exercises for any of the meta-model categories.

Experiment 7
Think of a current problem and write down a one-sentence description. Then reframe it as an opportunity. Spend a day noting each "problem" you come across and then write a positive reframe. (This can be mind-bending, so a day is more than long enough!)

Experiment 8
When a member of staff has a little moan about you, or a pupil, or the school, or life in general, have a go at articulating a positive reframe on the spot. Health warning: limit yourself, or you could get a reputation in the staffroom as an eternal optimist.

Experiment 9
Think of a situation with a pupil that you want to improve. Create a

metaphor that you could use with the child to gain the outcome you want through an unspoken message. Be clear of the outcome you want and choose a style of telling appropriate to the pupil. Make sure you match all the key elements of the real situation with a metaphoric one. As you tell the meaphor, you can use Milton abstract language to create a repetitive state of mind for some embedded commands to begin the improvment process. Notice the effects of these over time.

Experiment 10

Listen for a student who, at an appropriate time, makes a strong belief statement linked to a piece of "faulty logic" such as "You're a terrible teacher because you say mean things." Practise using the sleight-of-mouth strategies to change the belief and bring them out of that particular constraining box. This becomes easier with practice, so practise every time you have an opportunity! I'm not saying you'll be 100 per cent successful the first time, but the more you practise, the more likely you are to effect a change.

Experiment 11

Write yourself a number of visualising scripts, or mental rehearsals, to begin a lesson. They should be designed to expose the class to the desired future learning goals of the lesson by asking the students to imagine the end result and how they will feel about it, seeing it completed successfully.

Experiment 12

Write yourself a number of relaxation scripts that you could use at the end of a lesson to help the class process what they have learned (and to put them into a good learning state for the next lesson).

It takes a little while to adjust to these ways of speaking and working but you can certainly, now, go ahead and apply your learning in these experiments, in a way that is comfortable and natural for you.

General rules of engagement

Philip Waterhouse's (1990) advice on how best to speak to students still applies today: "Be simple; be short; be human." Although this is generally a good maxim, you know that departing from the first two instructions can be done to good effect when it is done deliberately and with a positive intention, as in the Milton model. For teachers, the third part will always need to be adhered to. Waterhouse gave other injunctions, which are confirmed by the NLP language approaches:

- Use concrete and behavioural nouns rather than abstract ones (nominalisations).
- Speak in the active voice rather than the passive.
- Use direct statements rather than circumlocutions.
- Keep the student and their behaviour in focus.

With the knowledge that has come out of the application of the NLP principles in the classroom, we can now extend and particularise these guidelines as follows:

Listen to their language
Remember that the different aspects of a pupil's language give you different sets of clues as to the child's mindset. What predicates does it contain – visual, auditory, kinaesthetic or neutral? Are these strengthened by what you can notice about the child's voice tone and pitch, rate of talking, gestures, breathing and so on? What is the most likely uppermost anxiety being expressed through this behaviour?

What logical level is the language pitched in? For instance:

- **Community:** This school is pathetic, making us do stupid things like graphs.
- **Identity:** I am useless at maths.
- **Beliefs/values:** I'll never learn how to do graphs/They are not important – when will I ever need to use graphs again?
- **Capability:** I just don't know how to even start doing a graph.
- **Behaviour:** When I draw a graph it goes all wrong/wonky.
- **Environment:** This classroom is too noisy/hot/cramped (to draw these graphs).

Do as they want/need to be done by!
One of the first books I read was Charles Kingsley's *The Water Babies*. All my life I have remembered the character, Mrs Doasyouwouldbedoneby, and considered that a name like that was a really good maxim to live by. Although it has, by and large, served me well, I now know that an even better guideline for improving relationships with other human beings is do to others in the way *they* want to be done unto. After all, as a unique human being, I am probably the only person in the world who wants to be done unto in exactly the way I want to be done unto! With that in mind, a prerequisite of management behaviour must be developing good information-gathering skills – improving your perceptual acuity to what makes the other person different and unique. This is about recognising and using the key meta-programs that the person is using to live in the world.

Say it as you want it to be!
Give positive directions, not negative commands. Everyone knows that any order that begins with *"don't"* is an invitation to the subconscious mind to do precisely what follows. Psychologists tell us that the subconscious mind cannot process the word "don't" consciously. It has first to consider and bring to the conscious part of our brain whatever follows this overworked word. Which is why the action is suited to the words *after* the "don't", and the very behaviour that was unwanted then appears – and appears to us as defiance. So this golden rule means that you direct your pupils to the behaviour you want to see them exhibit: "Jane, I want you to go back to your table" rather than "Jane, don't wander around the room."

However, as every parent of a very young child knows, "don't" is an excellent way of giving the child an instruction. This "negative psychology" approach of parents can be applied to older pupils by prefixing an instruction of what you want them to do with a negative: "Don't think you will find this easy." The unconscious mind will tend follow the words that come after the "don't". More examples of these speech patterns can be found in the section on embedded commands in Chapter Five.

"It ain't what you say, it's the way that you say it"
Although I have been stressing that what you say is important, this

song line is a commonly held truth because we know that vocal tone talks directly to the emotions. Talking in a harsh or sharp tone of voice to children who are auditory-tonal is likely to raise their anxiety levels and lower their self-esteem much more strongly than for children using the other systems. However, you can now extend this saying to include not just your choice of tone, but also your choice of vocabulary and sentence structure.

Construct your sentences carefully. Build in the presuppositions and then add the tones that will give you the response you want. The right choice of words expressed with a confident, expectant and positive tone, backed up by congruent body language and facial expression, is the most effective way of directing children's behaviour.

The different language approaches are used to pace where the child is in their behaviour and lead them to new behaviour. This generally follows the pattern:

1. Clean or nonviolent language and the meta-model questions to elicit and describe the problem behaviour;
2. Metaphoric language to open up the child's mindscape around the problem and to lead them towards the possibilities of new behaviours;
3. The Milton model to create and install the new behaviours into the child's mindset.

Negative and positive statements

The ways teachers linguistically manage the classroom can be classified into six strategies involving some form of positive or negative description of the behaviour. They have different levels of effectiveness.

If we define "positive" as a descriptor of a desired behaviour; and "negative" as that of an undesirable behaviour, then we have:

1. Negative only
There is too much noise in this room.
A negative statement alone lowers energy levels and raises negative feelings and therefore is not a recommended strategy.

2. Positive followed by a negative
I want you to listen – there is too much noise in this room.
The class will remember the last thing said more strongly then the first, so this, too, is a strategy to be avoided.

3. Negative followed by a positive
There's too much noise in this classroom – I want you to listen.
This is a powerful approach if the class is unaware of the inappropriate behaviour and the negative is said in an even tone of voice accompanied by neutral, nonverbal language.

4. Positive only
I need to have it quieter in here.
A really good approach if you have the right relationship with the class.

5. Positive followed by an even more positive statement
You are working nice and quietly and now I need it even quieter.
Pacing what they are doing and encouraging and leading them to an even higher goal.

6. Sandwich (positive and negative and followed by a positive)
You've been working really well – now, though, there's too much noise in the room, and I need to have it really quiet.
This raises energy levels and talks to both minds – the conscious and the unconscious.

Do you know your own relative use of these six?

In conclusion

I don't suppose you'll remember everything you have read at first. However, you will know that we have been talking about models, and you can experiment with their use. As the most powerful communication tools, the NLP language approaches change your conversations subtly, almost unconsciously, to get you better-behaved students, and I don't know yet whether, after reading this book, you are aware that you already know more at an unconscious level than you think you do.

You may be wondering how you will utilise what you have learned, although you will be pleasantly surprised as you discover how easily you can apply these new ideas and skills when dealing with your students.

You may, or you may not, be able to picture yourself in the future using these skills and it doesn't really have to be a big, clear picture, but it may just be right up there in front of you now to hold. Or you may have some other way of integrating these skills into your teaching. You may just feel your way gently into their use. And it doesn't matter which of these you do or whether you do them as I have laid them out. You can find your own way because they will all be beneficial, given that you do them for the sake of your students.

Bibliography

Anderson, J, 1993, *Thinking, Changing, Rearranging*, Metamorphous Press, Portland, OR.

Apter, T, 1997, *The Confident Child*, W W Norton, New York.

Arbinger Institute, 2000, *Leadership and Self-Deception: Getting Out of the Box*, Berrett-Koestler, San Francisco, CA.

Balbernie, R, 1998, *Infant–Parent Psychotherapy and Infant Mental Health: A Strategy for Early Intervention and Prevention*, Severn NHS Trust, Gloucester, UK.

Berliner, D, and Casanova, U, 1993, *Putting Research to Work in Your School*, SIRI/Skylight, Arlington Heights, IL.

Blackerby, D A, 1996, *Rediscover the Joy of Learning*, Success Skills, Oklahoma City, OK.

Bodenhamer, B G, and Hall, L M, 1997, *Figuring Out People: Design Engineering with Meta-Programs*, Crown House Publishing, Carmarthen, Wales.

Bryner A, and Markova, D, 1997, *An Unused Intelligence: Physical Thinking for 21st Century Leadership*, Conari Press, Berkeley, CA.

Canter, L, and Canter, M, 1992, *Assertive Discipline: Positive Behaviour Management for Today's Classroom*, Canter and Associates, Santa Monica, CA.

Carter, R, 1998, *Mapping the Mind*, Weidenfield and Nicolson, London.

Csikszentmihalyi, M, 1997, *Creativity: Flow and the Psychology of Discovery and Invention*, HarperCollins, New York.

Curry, N E, and Johnson, C N, 1990, *Beyond Self Esteem*, The National Association for the Education of Young Children, Washington, DC.

De Bono, Edward, 1982, *Lateral Thinking for Management: A Handbook*, Pelican Books, Middlesex, England.

Dhority, L, 1991, *The ACT Approach: The Use of Suggestion for Integrative Learning*, Gordon and Breach Science Publishers, SA.

Dilts, R, 1990, *Changing Belief Systems with NLP*, Meta Publications, Capitola, CA.

Dilts, R, 2001, *Sleight of Mouth*, Meda Publications, Capitola, CA.

Dreikurs, Rudolf, *Child Guidance and Education collected papers*, 1984.

Dryden, G, and Vos, J, 1994, *The Learning Revolution*, Accelerated Learning Systems, Aylesbury, Bucks.

Elton, Lord, 1989, *Discipline in Schools*, Report of the Committee of Enquiry chaired by Lord Elton. HMSO, London.

Gardner, H, 1983, *Frames of Mind: The Theory of Multiple Intelligences*, Basic Books, New York.

Glasser, W, 1998, *Choice Theory in the Classroom*, Harper Perennial, New York.

Gordon, G, 1996, *Managing Challenging Children*, Prim-Ed Publishing, Greenwood, Western Australia.

Grinder, M, 1991, *Righting the Educational Conveyor Belt*, Metamorphous Press, Portland, OR.

Haddawy, H (tr.), 1990, *The Arabian Nights*, M. Mahdi (ed.), W W Norton & Co., New York.

Hall, L M, and Bodenhamer, B G, 1997, *Mind-Lines: Lines for Changing Minds – The Magic of Conversational Reframing*, ET Publications, Grand Junction, CO.

Hannaford, C, 1995, *Smart Moves: Why Learning is Not All in Your Head*, Great Ocean Publishing, Arlington, VA.

Hayes, D, 1998, *Effective Verbal Communication*, Hodder & Stoughton, London.

Hein Piet, 2002, *Collected Grooks I*, Borgen Forlag, Copenhagen, Denmark.

Heron, J, 1989, *The Facilitator's Handbook*, Kogan Page, London.

Hill, F, and Parsons, L, 2000, *Teamwork in the Management of Emotional Behavioural Difficulties*, David Fulton, London.

Holt, J, 1964, *How Children Fail*, Pitman, New York.

Hook, P, and Vass, A, 2000, *Confident Classroom Leadership*, David Fulton, London.

Jacobsen, S, 1983, *Meta-Cation: Prescriptions for Some Ailing Educational Processes*, Meta Publications, Cupertino, CA.

Jasmine, J, 1996, *Teaching with Multiple Intelligences*, Teacher Created Materials, Westminster, CA.

Jensen, E, 1994, *The Learning Brain*, Turning Point Publishing, San Diego, CA.

Jensen, E, 2000, *Music with the Brain in Mind*, Brain Store Inc., San Diego, CA.

Kazantzakis, Nikos, 1952, 2000, *Zorba The Greek*, FF Classics, Faber and Faber, London.

Kilman, K W, 1992, Conflict and Negotiation Processes in Organisations, in *Handbook of Industrial and Organisational Psychology*, 2nd ed., Consulting Psychologists Press, Palo Alto, CA.

Kinder, K et al., 1999, *Raising Behaviour: A School View*, NFER, Slough.

Kingsley, Charles, 1995, *The Water Babies*, Puffin Classics.

Lawley, J, and Tompkins, P, 2000, *Metaphors in Mind: Transformation Through Symbolic Modelling*, Developing Company Press, London.

Le Doux, J, 1999, *The Emotional Brain*, Phoenix, London.

Lewis, N, 1994, *The Book of Babel: Words and the Way We See Things*, Viking, London.

Lozanov, G, 1979, *Suggestology and Outlines of Suggestopedia*, Gordon and Breach Publishers, New York.

MacGrath, M, 1998, *The Art of Teaching Peacefully: Improving Behaviour and Reducing Conflict in the Classroom*, David Fulton Pub., London.

Maines, B, and Robinson, G, 1991, *Teacher Talk*, Lucky Duck Publishing, Bristol.

McCarthy, B, and Morris, S, 1995, *4-MAT in Action: Sample Units for Grades 7–12*, About Learning Inc, Chicago.

McDermot, I, and Jago, W, 2001, *The NLP Coach*, Piatkus, London.

Mills, R W, 1980, *Classroom Observation of Primary School Children*, Unwin Education Books, London.

Montgomery, D, 1989, *Managing Behaviour Problems*, Hodder & Stoughton, London.

National Advisory Committee on Creative and Cultural Education (NAC-CCE), 1999, *All Our Futures: Creativity, Culture and Education*, National Advisory Committee on Creative and Cultural Education, a Department for Education and Skills publication, Sudbury, Suffolk.

Pinker, S, 1994, *The Language Instinct: A New Science of Language and Mind*, Penguin, London.

Polanyi, M, 1967, *The Tacit Dimension*, Routledge, London.

Porter, L, 2000, *Behaviour in Schools: Theory and Practice for Teachers*, Open University Press, Buckinghamshire.

Richmond, P, 1970, *An Introduction to Piaget*, Routledge & Kegan Paul, London.

Rogers, W A, 1992, *Managing Teacher Stress*, Pitman, London.

Rogers, W, 1994, *Behaviour Recovery: A Whole School Programme for Mainstream Schools*, Longman, Harlow, Essex.

Rosenberg, M B, 1999, *Non-violent Communication: A Language of Compassion*, PuddleDancer Press, Encinitas, CA.

Senge, P, 1994, *The Fifth Discipline Fieldbook*, Nicholas Brealey Pub., London.

Senge, P et al., 2000, *Schools That Learn*, Nicholas Brealey, London.

Sharron, H, and Coulter, M, 1994, *Changing Children's Minds: Feuerstein's Revolution in the Teaching of Intelligence*, Imaginative Minds, Birmingham.

Sharvet, S R, 1997, *Words That Change Minds: Mastering the Language of Influence*, Kendall Hunt, Dubuque, Iowa.

Shaw, S, and Hawes, T, 1998, *Effective Teaching and Learning in the Primary Classroom: A Practical Guide to Brain Compatible Learning*, The SERVICES Ltd., Leicester.

Sklare, G B, 1997, *Brief Counseling that Works: A Solution-Focused Approach for School Counselors*, Corwin Press, Thousand Oaks, CA.

Stewart, P, 2002, My Best Teacher, *Times Educational Supplement*, 29 March.

Vygotsky, L S, 1962, *Thought and Language*, MIT Press, Cambridge, MA.

Waterhouse, P, 1990, *Classroom Management*, Network Educational Press, Stafford, UK.

Wilber, K, 2001, *A Brief History of Everything*, Shambhala Publications, Boston.

Yen Mah, A, 2000, *Watching The Tree*, HarperCollins, London.